Hike the
Santa Barbara
Backcountry

Hike the Santa Barbara Backcountry

A Hiker's Guide to the
Southern Los Padres
National Forest

Dennis R. Gagnon

Western Tanager Press
Santa Cruz

Cover design by Lynn Piquett
Cartography by Lynn Piquett
Photographs by the author unless otherwise noted
Typography by TypaGraphix

ISBN: 0-934136-36-x
Library of Congress Card Catalog Number 81-50166
Printed in the United States of America

Western Tanager Press
1111 Pacific Ave.
Santa Cruz, CA 95060

DEDICATION

This Third Edition of "Hiking the Santa Barbara Backcountry" is dedicated to E.R. "Jim" Blakley.

Jim Blakley was born in Denver, Colorado in 1924. An inveterate hiker, Jim earned his trail legs exploring the Rockies and their foothills during his elementary and high school years. After an interruption for service in World War II he moved south to Tempe to study botany at Arizona State University. After completing his studies, he went on to work as an assistant at the Desert Botanical Garden.

In 1956, Jim and his wife moved to Santa Barbara where he was employed as the superintendent of the local botanical garden. He has since gone on to become the Grounds Superintendent for the Goleta School District. Soon after his move to Santa Barbara, Jim took to the roads and trails of the Los Padres National Forest. In the course of his hikes he came across numerous Indian and pioneer ruins and discovered that even local experts knew little of the history connected with these early settlements. Thus was born Jim's hobby as chronicler of the history of the Santa Barbara Backcountry. His work has grown from a few pages in a single notebook to an entire archive containing well over a hundred volumes and many rare and priceless old photographs. The archive also contains hours of taped interviews with all the living descendants of the original backcountry settlers.

Jim has always been most generous with his research, happily sharing the fruits of his work even with total strangers. He frequently is a guest speaker at lectures and slide shows on local history and often volunteers to lead introductory hikes into the nearby backcountry. He was further a co-founder of the Los Padres Interpretive Association, whose purpose is to educate the public about the natural history of the forest. Were it not for Jim, much of the early chronicle of this corner of California would today be lost. For his detailed work and his spirit of giving, we are all in his debt. It is for this reason that I dedicate the third edition of this guide to him.

To that greatest of winged creatures,
The California Condor;
Who, together with all animals and mountains,
All forests and streams,
Seeks a new covenant of understanding with man:
That man, understanding of their habits and their height,
Their vastness and their melody,
Might see an order far beyond his own
And again realize the joy of being creature,
Instead of creator.
That he might read
In the sternness of a great bird's gaze,
In the freedom of its flight
And the grace of its glide
The message:
That he who lives by the sword shall perish by the sword;
Whether that sword be
Civilized,
Mechanized,
Or rationalized.

Reyes Creek, December 1973

You are riding up a trail at sunset, twenty miles from the nearest human settlement, and you see racing toward you out of the Sun's disc a great dark spot growing larger and larger with incredible speed. Suddenly he looms above you, peering down with an age-old rather remote gaze. His eyes seem to have seen so much more than men that he appears only mildly interested. To feel the presence of that vast composure and to hear the rush and whistle of his feathers through the air, and to see him gone to his home in the darkening east having passed within a rope's cast of you is something to be forever remembered.

Dick Smith

CONTENTS

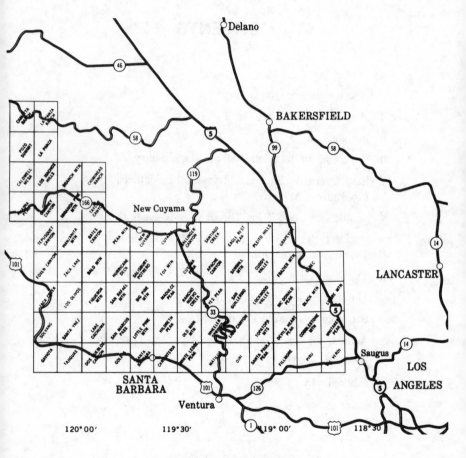

**INDEX TO 7½ MINUTE
QUADRANGLE MAPS**

ACKNOWLEDGEMENTS

I am again grateful to Russ Leadabrand and Joseph Simon, who, nearly 15 years ago, gave me the confidence and inspiration to write the first edition of this guide. Since then, many others have come along to help me keep it up to date and in print. I am also very grateful to Hal Morris, my publisher, a man of unusual patience, and to Michael Gant, my very competent editor, for their interest in this third edition.

Throughout the years, I have leaned heavily on the good people of the U.S. Forest Service to keep me up to date. From their ranks, I want especially to thank Sam Alfano, former Recreation Management Officer, and Ed Gornowski, his successor, for their time and trouble. John Boggs of the Ojai District was very helpful on keeping me informed about changes resulting from the severe fires in recent years.

Much of my historical data was obtained through Bob Burtness and the Boy Scouts of America, the late Dick Smith, the files of the *Santa Barbara News-Press,* the Santa Barbara Museum of Natural History, and the Ojai Museum, but it was Jim Blakley who helped me organize the whole picture and put it into perspective. Linda Powers, as always, kept the project on target. Thanks also to John Korb, Philip Woodard, Donna Jean Steines, Carol Lasky, and David of Sespe Creek.

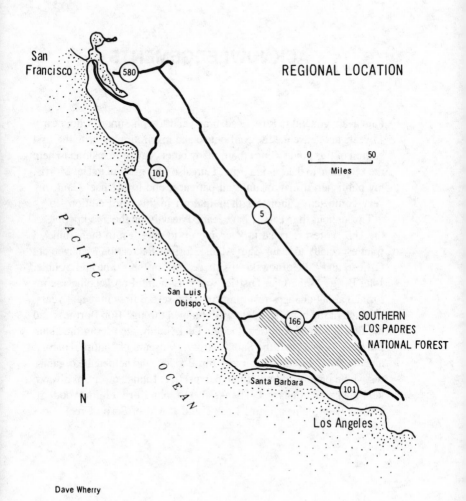

San
Francisco

REGIONAL LOCATION

580

0   50
Miles

101

5

PACIFIC

San Luis
Obispo

N

166

SOUTHERN
LOS PADRES
NATIONAL FOREST

OCEAN

Santa Barbara

101

Los Angeles

Dave Wherry

Location of the Santa Barbara Backcountry

I
HOW TO USE THIS GUIDE

This guide is divided into four sections: (1) 32 easy trip suggestions varying in length from a couple of hours to overnight; (2) 23 backpack trips into the wildest part of the Santa Barbara Backcountry lasting as long as a week; (3) detailed directions to all 117 trail camps in the Southern Los Padres National Forest; and (4) driving directions to each of the roadheads from which the hikes begin.

The two chapters of trip suggestions will give you overall information on many of the different hiking areas and outline some of my own favorite routes. The trail camps chapter will provide you with details on the size of each camp, water availability, vegetation, fishing possibilities, and fire closures; in short, everything you could possibly want to know about the camp and its environs.

In the detailed trip suggestions, the driving directions include just the relevant roadheads from which to start. Complete information on how to reach the roadheads is contained in the roadheads chapter, which is arranged alphabetically.

I recommend studying the trip suggestions first. Then as you grow more familiar with the Santa Barbara Backcountry, use the chapter on trail camps (also alphabetical) to plan your own excursions into this million-acre primitive region. Take this book with you on your trip and use it for directions to your destination, as a guide to alternative trail camps, to locate swimming holes, archeological sites, and pioneer ruins, and to help identify plants, trees and land forms.

INFORMATION YOU SHOULD KNOW

SEASONAL FIRE CLOSURES: Because of the extreme summertime fire danger in Southern California, portions of the Los Padres

National Forest are subject to a seasonal fire closure. The areas affected change from year to year, largely depending upon the density and dryness of the chaparral. These areas are generally closed from July 1 to the first heavy winter rains. An up-to-date map of the areas affected in any given year may be obtained free at any district ranger station. Those trail camps and trip suggestions in areas traditionally affected by this closure are designated in the text by the notion "F/C."

FIRE PERMIT: Regulations governing the necessity of possessing a permit to build backcountry campfires or use portable gas stoves have changed in recent years. These regulations are still in a state of flux. Briefly: you *must* always have a fire permit to camp in the San Rafael or Dick Smith wilderness areas and you *must* have a permit to camp in *other* backcountry areas between May 15 and October 31. But since the rules will probably change, and since permits are free and easy to obtain, it's wise to get one regardless. Stop in at a district ranger station or at the U.S.F.S. headquarters in Goleta.

In the San Rafael and Dick Smith wilderness areas, you must camp *only* at designated trail camps and build your fire, subject to regulations, in the stoves provided. Outside these wilderness areas, you may bivouac and build a fire outside designated trail camps subject to the provisions of your campfire permit.

WILDERNESS PERMITS: Wilderness permits are no longer required to camp in the wilderness areas of the Santa Barbara Backcountry. But this regulation, too, may change in the future. In the event it does, I have provided the notation "W/A" throughout the text for trail camps and trips which would be affected.

LICENSES: Many people travel into the backcountry to fish or hunt. In each case, a valid license must be in your possession according to state law. The better fishing streams are noted throughout the text. They are, generally speaking, the larger streams, which do not dry out in summer. Most streams are not stocked.

WEATHER: Except during the stormy winter and the sizzling summer months, the weather of the Santa Barbara Backcountry is usually mild. Every experienced hiker, however, knows the importance of always being properly protected against the elements. Temperatures in the high country can drop below freezing almost any month of the year, and winter snowstorms can cause blizzard conditions to occur at high elevations. Be sure to bring along a warm sleeping bag and jacket as well as rain protection. Be aware that winter rains can make stream crossings impassable. Unpredictable warm weather thundershowers can cause flash flooding in summer. Spring runoff from high mountain slopes can likewise make stream crossings treacherous.

It is always wise to obtain an extended weather forecast before leaving on a backcountry trek. District ranger stations (see page 175 for telephone numbers) often will have up-to-date information.

HIKES: To help you understand the degree of difficulty in the hikes I describe, I use the following rule of thumb: "easy" refers to a route that involves an altitude gain or loss of less than 500 feet per mile; a "moderate" trail climbs or decends an average of 500 feet to 1,000 feet per mile; a "strenuous" or "steep" hike is anything with a gain of more than 1,000 feet per mile.

Trail conditions naturally have some effect on the rating that I have given to a particular route.

TRAILS AND FIRE ROADS: Trails are clearly visible and generally easy-to-follow pathways through the backcountry. Fire roads are dirt, jeep, or maintenance roads that have been permanently closed to public auto traffic. Many of these roads are hiking routes, and some have become "designated two-wheel vehicle routes" (motorcycle trails). Some, if not many of the trails and fire roads of the Santa Barbara Backcountry are well signed and easily followed. Since many of them are marked with signs that show only their Forest Service code number (for example, 8NO2), I have noted these numbers throughout the text.

MOUNTAIN BIKES: There are those who say that mountain bikes are becoming a nuisance on the fire roads and trails of the Santa Barbara Backcountry. They maintain that their tires erode the landscape, that their speed is a menace to hikers, and that their riders are often daredevil and inconsiderate. Mountain bike enthusiasts, on the other hand, defend their sport as merely a high-tech extension of man's use of the mountains, and insist that, since their bikes are human-powered, they deserve their place in the backcountry. While I will not use these pages as a podium for either position, I will tell you that I have very nearly been run down by bicyclists speeding recklessly down some fire roads, and I would warn hikers to be extra alert for the possibility of such encounters. Current U.S.F.S. regulations permit mountain bikes on the roads and trails of the Los Padres. *But* mountain bikes are specifically banned from entrance into the San Rafael or Dick Smith wilderness areas.

MAPS: You should carry two different maps with you when hiking in the Santa Barbara Backcountry: a current U.S. Forest Service Recreation map *and* a topographic map. The former is available from any district ranger station for a small fee and shows the latest changes in routes, trail camps, and fire closures. Forest Service maps also show the code number for each backcountry road and trail. Topographic maps are a valuable tool for the hiker because they depict the landscape in three dimensions through the use of contour lines. Topographic maps are published by the U.S. Geological Survey and are available at Southern California mountain and map shops. They are also sold at many district ranger stations. A notation of the topographic map quadrangles needed for each hike in this book is made after its route description following the term "TOPO." All topographic maps for this region are in the 7½ minute series. Always carry a compass for use with these maps.

TRAIL CAMPS: A trail camp is a backcountry site with one or more stoves and/or tables provided by the Forest Service for picnicking or overnight camping. The number of stoves at a trail camp will give you an idea of its size. A camp with three stoves, for example, has room for three parties of campers. Accessible only by foot or on horseback (a few can be reached by motorcycle), a *trail camp* is distinct from a *campground,* which is accessible by normal passenger car.

Most camps are located near reliable water sources—streams or springs. Some are along "seasonal" or "intermittent" creeks that run only during the wet months. Be aware, though, that even the most dependable stream may cease to flow in an unusually dry year. Without exception, spring, early summer, and late fall are the best times to visit these camps.

Trail camp listings include complete guidelines for reaching the camp from the nearest roadhead and an idea of the facilities offered. The altitude of each camp is given in parentheses following its name. *One-way* mileage from roadhead to camp follows the elevation, also in parentheses.

II

INTRODUCTION
THE LAND

Extending east and north from the coastal city of Santa Barbara is a vast backcountry of nearly one million acres that is rich in geological, Indian, and pioneer history. Bounded on the east by Interstate 5 and on the north by State Highway 166, the southern division of the Los Padres National Forest includes major portions of Ventura and Santa Barbara counties, much of it less than two hours by car from downtown Los Angeles. Most of this area receives relatively little use and it has much to offer. This is the Santa Barbara Backcountry.

The land in this corner of California lay for millenia beneath the sea until over a million years ago great forces along the San Andreas Fault caused it to rise, buckle, and fold. The ocean retreated, revealing a vast landscape of contorted sandstone, shale, and conglomerate rock. Time, wind, and erosion have worn these mountains to their present pattern of rugged canyons and craggy peaks. And the mountains are still moving, still growing, still changing. The active Santa Ynez, Big and Little Pine, Nacimiento, and mighty San Andreas faults run through and around this corner of our state. Several quakes of noticeable size occur annually.

Two extensive mountain ranges meet in the Santa Barbara Backcountry. The Transverse Ranges begin with the Santa Ynez Mountains and extend from here to include the San Gabriel, San Bernardino, and San Jacinto ranges. The Coastal Ranges also begin here and extend north as far as Alaska.

Water, borne in from the Pacific by winter storms and spring showers has always played an important role in the shaping of the slopes, the deposition of soil, and the spread of life in this region. Many of the

5

THE SOUTHERN LOS PADRES
NATIONAL FOREST

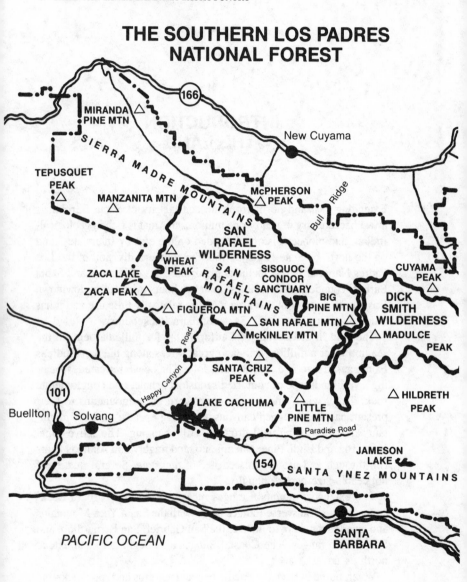

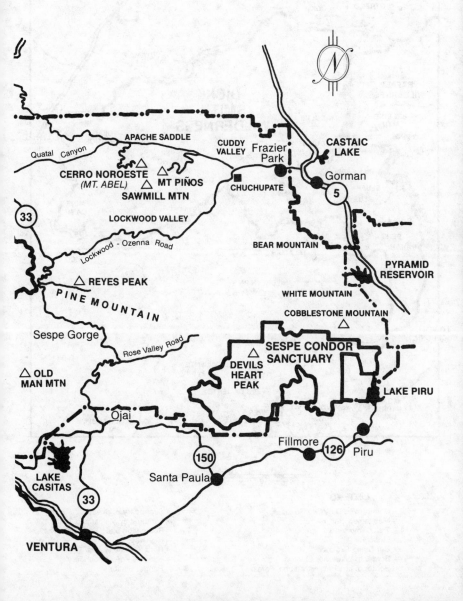

THE DICK SMITH WILDERNESS AND ENVIRONS

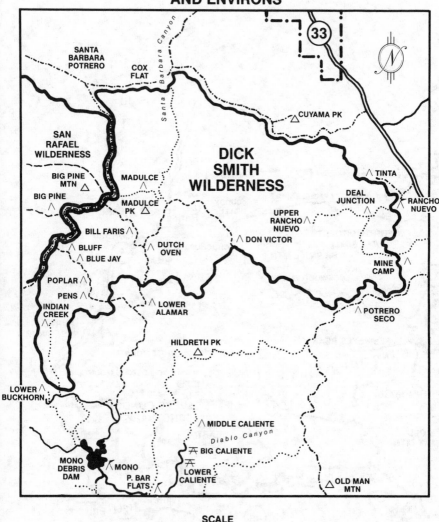

SCALE

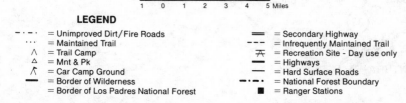

1   0   1   2   3   4   5 Miles

LEGEND

- – · – · = Unimproved Dirt/Fire Roads
- · · · = Maintained Trail
- ∧ = Trail Camp
- △ = Mnt & Pk
- ⋀ = Car Camp Ground
- = Border of Wilderness
- = Border of Los Padres National Forest

- = Secondary Highway
- – – – = Infrequently Maintained Trail
- 〒 = Recreation Site - Day use only
- — = Highways
- — = Hard Surface Roads
- – · · – = National Forest Boundary
- ■ = Ranger Stations

streams which drain the numerous subranges in the forest have cut deep chasms into the soft sedimentary soils. The dense chaparral carpeting the lower slopes here acts as a sponge to control runoff during the rainy season (November to May) into the riparian woodlands of the canyons, where live oaks, sycamores, alders, and other water-loving species attempt to keep the canyon streambeds in check. On the higher ridges, where snow falls in winter, extensive forests of conifers absorb the slowly melting, life-giving moisture. By cool wet winters, nature controls flooding and guarantees an adequate water supply for the hot, dry summers. At least in most years.

The chaparral is the most noticeable vegetation. From the conifer belt down to sea level, manzanita, scrub oak, ceonothus, chamise, sage, yucca, and similar species form an elfin forest of dwarfed trees and hardy brush leading a spartan existence on the nutrient-poor soil. The canyons host a stream woodland that favors water-loving live oaks, laurels, sycamores, alders, willows, and maples. On some lower slopes, bigcone spruce, digger, coulter, and piñon pines, thrive; higher up, white fir, ponderosa, jeffrey, and sugar pines raise their lofty boughs skyward. And in the spring, everywhere occurs that mystical transformation of dry brushland into lush grasses jeweled with wildflowers. Many of the high ridges, especially in the Sierra Madre Range, are a brilliant mass of color at that time.

This unspoiled backcountry is the favorite haunt of many different animals, albeit in greatly reduced numbers than in Indian times. The skunk, gopher, weasel, mouse, bushtit, and sparrow live among the seemingly inhospitable chaparral, but most animals will be encountered in or near the canyons where the waters flow. Mule deer, raccoon, ring-tailed cat, squirrel, fox, rabbit, badger, and coyote are year-round residents in these lowlands. The few black bear, mountain lion, and bobcat remaining range here and higher up into the conifer belt, where woodpeckers, jays, owls, and swallows make their homes. High among the craggy ridges—in caves and among clefts—the golden and bald eagle, turkey vulture, hawk, and the endangered condor make their areas. The wary rattlesnake, its harmless cousins, and lizards, are found everywhere, though they prefer the canyons. In the larger streams, brown and golden trout (both native and stocked), salamanders, frogs, and turtles dwell. All of these animals are wild and have wisely learned

THE SAN RAFAEL WILDERNESS
AND SURROUNDING AREA

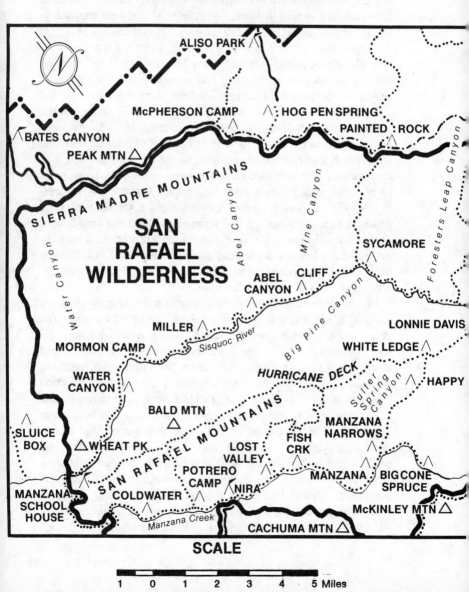

SCALE

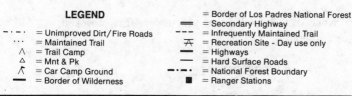

LEGEND

- · - · - = Unimproved Dirt / Fire Roads
· · · = Maintained Trail
∧ = Trail Camp
△ = Mnt & Pk
⋏ = Car Camp Ground
— = Border of Wilderness

= Border of Los Padres National Forest
= Secondary Highway
- - - = Infrequently Maintained Trail
⋔ = Recreation Site - Day use only
= Highways
— = Hard Surface Roads
- · - · - = National Forest Boundary
■ = Ranger Stations

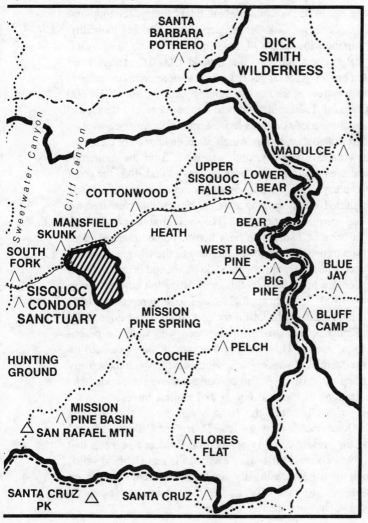

to fear man. None of them will harm you, unless first provoked, frightened, or cornered.

THE PEOPLE

Man has long inhabited the Santa Barbara Backcountry. Ten thousand years ago, the aboriginal Oak Grove People were building their dirt-banked huts in the wide valleys of the Sisquoc and Santa Ynez rivers. Archeological evidence suggests that around 1500 B.C., these tribes evolved from hunter-gatherer societies into a more complex culture, utilizing the resources of the sea and hunting game far inland. By 600 B.C., the Chumash Indians had arrived on the scene and developed one of the most advanced cultures in western North America with an enviable degree of sophistication. Much has been learned of their proficiency in weapons, basketry, and stonework from the numerous archeological sites discovered in these mountains and along the coast during this century. Family groups lived in circular-framed, thatched huts with a shared sweathouse or *temescal* nearby that was used for relaxation and spiritual rejuvenation. They ventured to sea on plank canoes called *tomols,* fished wth bent hooks, hunted marine mammals, and even traded with tribes as far away as the Channel Islands. They developed a monetary system based on shells, and in many places, some of which are mentioned in this book, they left cave paintings (pictographs) to baffle anthropologists and to inspire backcountry travelers. These amazingly beautiful rock paintings were undoubtedly created by Chumash shamans, medicine men who were the practitioners of tribal magic. These mysterious symbols were painted on the sandstone interiors of remote backcountry caves, which most likely served as religious shrines. Anthropologists believe the pictographs were visualizations of mystical beings and natural forces.

The first contact between the Indians and western civilization occurred in October of 1542 when Juan Rodriguez Cabrillo dropped anchor near the present-day city of Ventura. Evidence suggests that the meeting was cordial, gifts were exchanged, and Cabrillo sailed on. Although the tribe occasionally sighted a few other "houses on the sea," the Spanish essentially ignored their claims to New Spain for the next two and one-quarter centuries.

In the late 1760s, amid rumors of encroachment by the English and Russians in Alta California, the government in Mexico City decided that its holdings needed further exploration. Thus it was that Don Gaspar de Portola was appointed military governor of the region and authorized to lead an expedition to establish settlements in the new territory. Entering what was to become Ventura and Santa Barbara counties, Portola followed the coastal route along the southern edge of the Santa Ynez Mountains, and it was here that he first encountered the Chumash. These strong, inventive people, described by Franciscan missionaries as being "extremely intelligent and skillful, alert, and rather bold," survived the rigors of Christianity, civilization, and the mission system for less than half a century before their culture died out. Although descendants of the Chumash remain, the tribe's customs, language, traditions and insight have largely been lost. The missions reached the height of their influence during the 1820s, but the coming of Mexican independence, the granting of large land grants by the government to retiring soldiers, and the eventual secularization of the missions ensured their decline.

At about this same time, the Gold Rush brought all manner of pioneers to this country. Prospecting was common along many of the larger streams, especially Piru and Lockwood creeks, where relics of the era—sluice boxes, rusting pipes, and cabin ruins—are occasionally encountered. After the gold fever subsided, many of the drifters, tempted by cheap land and virgin countryside, decided to remain. pioneers like Jose Flores and Josiah T. Montgomery used their farming skills to settle down and cultivate high country meadows. Other homesteads sprang up in many of the hospitable regions of the backcountry. On the rich flatlands that surround these mountains, extensive ranches became common. Other men, such as Hiram Preservéd Wheat, who led a group of faith healers into the Sisquoc Valley in the 1880s to found a religious commune, settled in the larger canyons.

At the bequest of local communities concerned about the dangers of wildfire and erosion, the federal government entered the picture in 1898 when President William McKinley withdrew over one million acres of this backcountry into the Pine Mountain and Zaca Lake reserves. These lands were added to another withdrawal by President Theodore Roosevelt in 1908 to form the Santa Barbara National Forest.

VENTURA COUNTY'S PINE MOUNTAIN RECREATION AREA

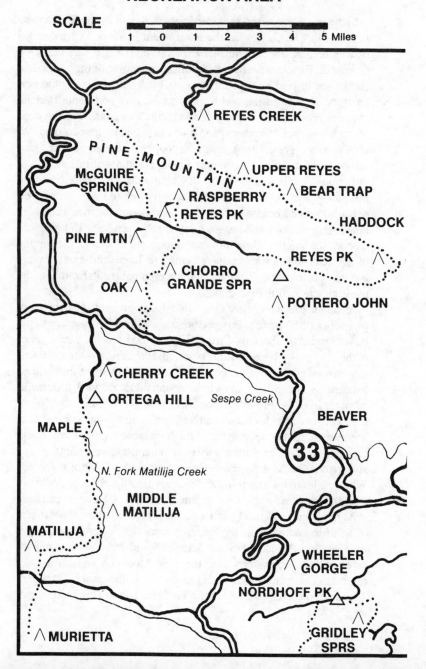

SCALE

1 0 1 2 3 4 5 Miles

REYES CREEK

PINE MOUNTAIN

UPPER REYES

BEAR TRAP

McGUIRE SPRING

RASPBERRY

REYES PK

HADDOCK

PINE MTN

REYES PK

CHORRO GRANDE SPR

OAK

POTRERO JOHN

CHERRY CREEK

ORTEGA HILL

Sespe Creek

BEAVER

MAPLE

33

N. Fork Matilija Creek

MIDDLE MATILIJA

MATILIJA

WHEELER GORGE

NORDHOFF PK

MURIETTA

GRIDLEY SPRS

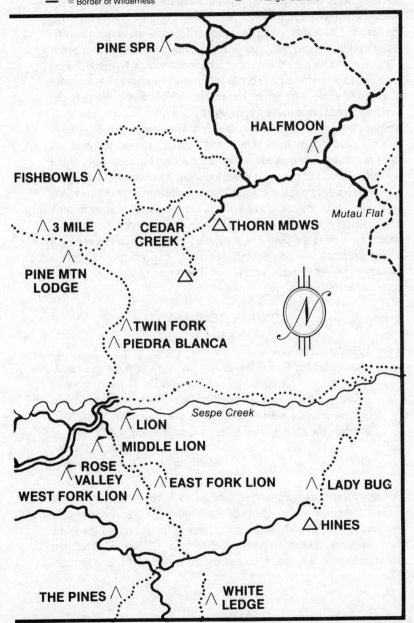

LEGEND

- – · – · = Unimproved Dirt/Fire Roads
- · · · = Maintained Trail
- ∧ = Trail Camp
- △ = Mnt & Pk
- ⼊ = Car Camp Ground
- ━━━ = Border of Wilderness
- ═══ = Border of Los Padres National Forest
- ══ = Secondary Highway
- – – – = Infrequently Maintained Trail
- ⊼ = Recreation Site - Day use only
- ━ = Highways
- — = Hard Surface Roads
- – · – · = National Forest Boundary
- ■ = Ranger Stations

PINE SPR ∧

HALFMOON ⼊

FISHBOWLS ∧

∧ 3 MILE

△ CEDAR CREEK

△ THORN MDWS

Mutau Flat

∧ PINE MTN LODGE

△

∧ TWIN FORK
∧ PIEDRA BLANCA

Sespe Creek

⼊ LION

⼊ MIDDLE LION

⼊ ROSE VALLEY

∧ EAST FORK LION

∧ LADY BUG

WEST FORK LION ∧

△ HINES

THE PINES ∧

∧ WHITE LEDGE

After additional boundary changes in 1938, the parcel was renamed the Los Padres National Forest to commemorate the Franciscan fathers.

Times have changed for these mountains. From untrammeled countryside, they have entered an age when wilderness areas must be officially designated and many ancient footpaths have evolved to modern highways. No longer an unknown backcountry, this National Forest is valued as a watershed and crude oil producer instead of as a source of gold and game. More than four million people now come here annually for recreation and escape. Most of the mines and homesteads are gone now, as are the ancient aboriginal dwellings, and such names as McDonald Cabin, Stone House, and Indian Cave refer to memories and time that seem strangely out of place today. But the magic of the wild places has not gone and these mountains have much of it. From windswept ridge to quiet canyon to mysterious pictograph dwells a power which is not easily grasped but can be deeply felt by anyone who will for a moment discard intellectual knowledge for intuitive observation. It is the power of a wildflower swaying in the wind, of a deer grazing on a dewy potrero at dawn, or an eagle soaring effortlessly in flight. It is a simple power. The power of things in balance. It is a peaceful power. And it is vast.

CONDOR COUNTRY

"Perhaps it is the rarity of the condor that lends a mysterious enchantment to the wilderness retreats over which the great birds soar. In these secluded places the condor is the symbol of wildness. Wilderness, with all its intangible meanings, seems to appear in its most tangible form when a condor is sighted, soaring effortlessly over some mountain stronghold."

Ian McMillan
Man and the California Condor

Perhaps most importantly of all, the Santa Barbara Backcountry is the last stronghold and sanctuary of one of our most grimly endangered species, the mighty California condor. Before the coming of the white man, condors ranged from Oregon to Baja California. The first documented sighting was recorded by the Lewis and Clark Expedition, along the Columbia River, in 1805. The spirit of Manifest Destiny that conquered the West, however, nearly wiped out the species. As early as the turn of the century, a significant decrease in the population was noticeable. The rifles of ranchers and cattlemen were largely to blame. It was then generally believed that the birds contributed to livestock losses, although this idea proved to be fallacious. Condors are strictly scavangers and *never* kill. The ignorance of hunters and egg collectors also helped to decimate the species.

Never numerous, the condor population had decreased so drastically by the late 1930s that concerned conservation groups managed to achieve some forms of protection. First, hunting of the birds was outlawed; then, in 1937, the Sisquoc Condor Sanctuary was established in what is now the San Rafael Wilderness. This 1,200-acre refuge within the Los Padres National Forest was joined by the 53,000-acre Sespe Sanctuary in 1947. Both areas feature rugged, inaccessible cliffs and clefts where condors are known to nest or forage.

Despite these measures, the condor population has continued to decline. At first, hunting laws were poorly enforced. Evidence also suggests that several big birds fell victim to secondary poisoning during federal rodent control programs in the San Joaquin Valley. Although laws are now more strongly enforced, any effort by the 27 (Summer, 1986) remaining condors to reestablish their numbers is complicated by their two-year reproductive cycle, which culminates in the hatching of only a single egg.

In a last-ditch effort to save the endangered species, the U.S. Fish and Wildlife Service established a captive breeding program in 1981. Under the plan, all mature adult condors will eventually be removed from the sanctuaries by wildlife experts. The birds will then be encouraged to breed in a controlled and predator-free environment, thus building up the species' numbers. In captivity, for example, a female bird can be convinced to lay up to three eggs per cycle merely by removing each egg from the clutch after it's laid. The young are then artifically incubated and raised in a safe environment to be eventually returned to the wild.

As of this writing, all but three condors have been removed from the wild to the breeding programs at the Los Angeles and San Diego zoos. Nearly a dozen have been hatched in captivity and three adolescents are scheduled for release this year. Although the Audubon Society has expressed some reservations about the program, it should be noted that scientists have managed to save other species—including the whooping crane, American bison, trumpeter swan, Pére David's deer—from extinction through captive breeding. Were it not for the program, the California condor almost certainly would soon become extinct.

Hikers should be aware that entry into the Sisquoc and Sespe sanctuaries, with the exception of the Sespe Creek Corridor, is illegal and strictly forbidden. Violators are subject to fine and imprisonment, and the laws are enforced by patrolling rangers. Since wild condors are adversely affected by human encroachment on their territory, anyone entering the sanctuaries may well be contributing to the extinction of the species. Hunters should know that all large dark birds, especially the condor, are protected by state game laws. Game wardens are always on patrol.

Fortune has indeed favored you if while hiking you are privileged to witness a condor in flight. Largest of all American land birds, with a wingspread that can exceed nine feet, this grand aviator is identified by white triangular patches under each wing and by an orange neck and head. Condors are able to soar without movement on the thermal air currents of the region farther and longer than any other bird. In motionless flight, in perfect balance with its natural environment, the condor surely is in rhythm with the heartbeat of wildness.

WILDERNESS AREAS OF THE SANTA BARBARA BACKCOUNTRY

The Southern Los Padres National Forest is unique not only as the last refuge of the California condor but also as the home of the first federal primitive area to be designated as an official wilderness. Here, within the 151,000 acres of the San Rafael Wilderness, true wildness reigns. Foot and stock trails, but no roads, are the only penetrations of civilization into this region of deep canyons, steep slopes, pine forests, and craggy summits. Elevations ranging from 1,200 to 6,596 feet offer every type of scenic variety. The Sisquoc River and Manzana Creek drain the watersheds of the lofty San Rafael and

Condors sun themselves on a ledge high above the backcountry.
(BUREAU OF SPORT FISHERIES AND WILDLIFE)

Sierra Madre Mountains and provide the primary access routes into the wild area. It was set aside in 1966, to be preserved forever in its undeveloped state, largely due to pressure brought to bear by local conservation groups and concerned citizens. Chief among these were Joy Parkinson of the Audubon Society, writer Robert Easton, and legendary conservationist and newspaperman Dick Smith.

Smith was born in Detroit Lakes, Minnesota, in 1929 and grew up traveling the plains of North Dakota with his father, who was a railroad engineer. In 1948 he moved to Santa Barbara and started work on the *News-Press* as a general assignment reporter. It was in the early 1950s that Smith was first introduced to the Santa Barbara Backcountry during a picnic on Figueroa Mountain with publisher Noel Young. While on a hike they took together that day, Dick's love for the Los Padres was kindled. He was to spend the rest of his life writing about, exploring, but above all striving to protect the wild unspoiled areas of Santa Barbara County. His last years were devoted to the struggle to save the California Condor. He was known as "the foremost protector of the Santa Barbara Backcountry." Dick died on February 2, 1977, while feeding his horses. Per his wishes, his ashes were scattered along that first trail he had hiked with Noel Young so many years before.

In Smith's obituary, friend and collaborator Robert Easton wrote: "Dick's concern for the total environment was unlimited . . . no trail—literally or figuratively—was too tough for him to take. He sat through committee meetings, attended the hearings, wrote the letters, made the calls, opened his door or came to your home at any hour of the day or night for a cause I can best sum up as life—life itself."

In 1984, Congress passed and President Reagan signed the California Wilderness Act, which set aside 64,700 acres west of Highway 33. Crowned by 6,541-foot Madulce Peak, harboring the many pools and waterfalls of Indian and Mono Creeks, and carpeted by a forest of conifers and chaparral, it was a region that Smith had long sought to preserve. On October 19, 1984, Anne Van Tyne of the Sierra CLub led a group of hikers into the backcountry to dedicate this new wild area as the Dick Smith Wilderness in his memory. It is only the third such wilderness area in California to be so named for an individual. Dick shares that honor with Ansel Adams and John Muir.

Newspaperman and conservationist Dick Smith, 1929–1977: "The foremost protector of the Santa Barbara Backcountry." (THE DICK SMITH ARCHIVES, COURTESY OF THE SANTA BARBARA MUSEUM OF NATURAL HISTORY.)

III

DAYHIKING IN THE SANTA BARBARA BACKCOUNTRY

For the newcomer to the Santa Barbara Backcountry, I have prepared the following series of dayhikes. Each explores a different region of the mountain landscape. They travel to mountain peaks, cool canyons, pleasant swimming holes, even to a local hot spring. These hikes range in distance from less than a half mile to more than ten miles and can be negotiated by the average hiker in good shape.

These day hikes can also be equally enjoyed by the seasoned veteran. If you live in the area, use one of them as a way to unwind after a hard day at work. If you're a weekend visitor to Santa Barbara, try to enrich your experience of this beautiful part of California by exploring its extraordinary mountain environment.

The first walks I offer you will be in and around the Santa Ynez Mountains right above town. I'll then branch out to some of the more far-flung portions of the Santa Barbara Backcountry.

An aerial view to the northeast of the rugged San Rafael Wilderness taken from high above the Sisquoc Condor Sanctuary. Sisquoc Canyon cuts left to right through the photograph. Logan Canyon is on the left. Judell Canyon is center right. In the distance is the Cuyama Badlands Area and, farther still, the outline of the southern Sierra Nevada. (U.S. FOREST SERVICE)

23

#1
THE JESUSITA TRAIL
TO INSPIRATION POINT
7 Miles Round Trip

Description: At over 1,800 feet in elevation, Inspiration Point offers the hiker a dramatic view out over Mission Canyon as well as the whole coastal plain of Santa Barbara. The mountain geography surrounding the point is no less impressive, with huge weathered sandstone slabs presided over by 3,333-foot Cathedral Peak. Come here on a clear windswept day. Bring a friend, a lunch, a book, or all three and plan for a delightful experience.

Driving: Roque Roadhead.

Directions: From the Cater Filtration Plant, hike onto the signed Jesusita Trail (22W17) near a plaque honoring legendary conservationist Dick Smith. As you travel easily along near San Roque Creek, there are seasonal pools that are fun to explore. The trail climbs a little away from the creek, then returns before reaching the private Morena Ranch 1.5 miles from the start. The Jesusita now begins climbing to the northeast up a tributary of San Roque, switchbacking through the chaparral to meet a power line maintenance road. Bearing left, the trail then follows that road to the unmarked turnoff for Inspiration Point, 3.5 miles from the start. Bear right here and head out to Inspiration Point, located at the east end of the hill where the road ends.

When you've been thoroughly inspired, return the way you came.
TOPO: *Santa Barbara*

#2
MISSION CANYON'S SEVEN FALLS
3 Miles Round Trip

Description. Maui may have its Seven Sacred Pools to which tourists swarm like mosquitoes to the unprotected flesh of the nearest backpacker. But Santa Barbara is blessed with its Seven Falls, which happily are visited largely only by the local hiking population. Don't expect to find solitude here on a warm spring weekend, just friendly camaraderie. Ever since the Santa Ynez Mountions rose high above the sea, water has cascaded down the chasm of Mission Canyon. The friction of water on sand has worn away and transformed the rugged rock into a series of falls, pools, and cascades that are a delight to enjoy.

Driving: Tunnel Roadhead.

Directions: Walk past a watertank and locked gate and continue along the Tunnel Fire Road. You soon cross Mission Creek on a sturdy bridge above the pool of little Fern Canyon Falls. Hike along on an uphill track to a shady junction under spreading live oaks. From here, the Tunnel Trail heads north up to the crest of East Camino Cielo, but your route continues straight ahead along the wide well-traveled Jesusita Trail (27W17), first up, then moderately downhill for 0.4 miles to Mission Creek. Boulderhop about 500 yards upstream through the gorge to the Seven Falls. If you do any climbing, exercise proper caution. There have been serious accidents among those who did not grant the slippery rock proper respect.
TOPO: *Santa Barbara*

#3
FROM SANTA BARBARA TO THE
SANTA YNEZ RIVER . . . THE HARD WAY
8.5 Miles One Way

Description: The easy way to get from Santa Barbara to the Santa Ynez River is to drive north on Highway 154 over San Marcos Pass and turn right onto the Paradise Road for a few miles. It's a pleasant drive, but the uphill tailgaters are annoying and the curvy road demands full attention. However, if you really want to savor the ruggedness of the Santa Ynez Mountains as well as enjoy magnificent views of Santa Barbara and its backcountry, you'll do it my way. From the edge of town, you'll climb up the Tunnel Trail to the top of the range near La Cumbre Peak. Then, from Angostura Pass, you'll descend via fire road and trail to the welcome coolness of the river. This is a rugged trip, so be sure to wear sturdy boots, get an early start, and pack along ample food and water.

Driving: This is a shuttle trip requiring two cars. Ideally, arrange for a group of friends to drive to the Santa Ynez Car Campground and pitch their tent at a choice site. Tell them you'll be arriving in camp for dinner. Then drive your car to the Tunnel Roadhead and take off on this daylong adventure to join them.

Description: Head off easily along Tunnel Road climbing slightly. You soon pass over gurgling Mission Creek and continue onto a signed junction a little more than a mile from the start. Turn right here onto the Tunnel Trail (27W14), so named because it roughly follows the route of the diversion tunnel supplying Santa Barbara with water from Gibraltar Dam. The trail climbs moderately, switchbacking steeply up through weathered sandstone formations whose starkness is softened by the ever-present chaparral. Hiking past some high tension power lines, your route meets a connector trail to Rattlesnake Canyon in 1.5 miles. Continue straight ahead, following the Tunnel Trail steeply uphill to the crest of the Santa Ynez Mountains, another 2 miles. No doubt reststops will be many, but use that opportunity to enjoy the increasingly expansive views of the coastal plain below. Once on top, relax, rest, and enjoy.

When it's time to continue, there are some encouraging facts to consider: Your views will now be into the rugged heart of the wild Santa Barbara Backcountry, you'll be traversing the cooler and more forested northern slopes of these mountains, and the going will be largely downhill. Cross East Camino Cielo and descend on Fireroad 5N25, which begins a short distance to the west. After you pass a locked gate, watch for the unsigned Tunnel Trail, which picks up on the left within the first quarter-mile. Follow this steeply descending pathway through chaparral for a mile to a junction with the Devil's Canyon Trail (27W21), which continues down to Gibraltar Dam. Bear left here onto the Mattias Potrero Trail (27W19) and follow it as it contours along the slope in and out of tributary canyons. Hike on a downhill track for 1.5 miles to Mattias Potrero Camp, set near a little meadow. In early season you can find streamwater and shade here.

When ready to resume the rest of your journey, head west a quarter-mile to a junction. Turn north on retiring jeep road 27W25 and walk the remaining mile down to the Santa Ynez River Road (5N18). After a refreshing dip in one of the river's many swimming holes, head west along the road to join your amazed friends at the campground.

I guarantee you will have a hearty appetite that night.

TOPOS: *Santa Barbara, Little Pine Mountain*

#4
A TREK DOWN RATTLESNAKE CANYON
2.8 Miles One Way

Description: Just the word "rattlesnake" seems forbidding and sends shivers down the spines of many people. But while I'm sure that some of these native reptiles inhabit this canyon in the Santa Ynez Mountains above Santa Barbara, I must confess I have never seen one here. In fact, this canyon is not forbidding at all; it's a delight to explore. On this hike you'll do just that as you travel across hillside and down canyon from the Gibraltar Road to the outskirts of town.

Driving: Start at Upper Rattlesnake Roadhead; end at Rattlesnake Roadhead.

Description: From the Gibraltar Road (5N25) descend moderately through the chaparral on a westerly bearing switchbacking down to a meadow on the edge of Rattlesnake Creek in 0.7 miles. This spot, locally known as Tin Can Cabin Flat, was named for a crude structure of poles and smashed five-gallon oil cans built early in the century here by one Bill O'Conner to prove up a homestead claim. The cabin is long gone.

There's a junction at this point. Ahead to the west is a connector path that travels over to the Tunnel Trail, but your route turns left and heads south along the bubbling creek. You soon pass through a shady narrows, then gain altitude above the stream hiking through an area of transplanted pines. A little less than a mile past the meadow, the trail switchbacks down the chaparral-covered hillside, crosses the creek, and joins an old dirt road. As you walk along, you'll notice to the right a number of footpaths made by use that travel into the brush. By all means take time to explore. Many lead to clear cool pools and small waterfalls that are delightful on a hot day.

When it's time to move on, continue down the dirt road to the car.

TOPO: *Santa Barbara*

#5
THE WEST FORK OF COLD SPRING CANYON
2 Miles One Way or Round Trip

Description: If I had but an hour or so on a busy day to sample the Santa Ynez Mountains behind Santa Barbara, I'd head up to Cold Spring Canyon. This little surprise off Mountain Drive behind Westmont College is easy to get to, the canyon is well-watered, and there are a number of waterfalls to be enjoyed. If you are indeed short on time, just hike the first mile up the west fork to the point where the trail begins to climb out of the canyon. But if you have the day off, and I hope you do, try the complete trip to sample both chaparral slopes and cool canyon.

Driving: Start at Lower Cold Spring Roadhead and finish at Upper Cold Spring; or just use Lower Cold Spring if you plan to backtrack.

Directions: Walk easily up the shady canyon along the creek for 0.3 miles to the point where the East and West Forks of Cold Spring Creek converge. Just downstream from this point, look for two large boulders which mark the trail junction and cross the creek. Continue up the West Fork at your leisure. At the point where the trail begins climbing out of the canyon you can get a great view of a 60-foot waterfall by boulder-hopping a short way upstream.

From this junction, the trail switchbacks through chaparral the remaining mile to the shuttle point on Gibraltar Road.

TOPO: *Santa Barbara*

#6
AN EASY CLIMB OF LA CUMBRE PEAK
0.3 Miles Round Trip

Description: At 3,985 feet, La Cumbre Peak is hardly the highest point in the Santa Ynez Mountains, and some might argue that so easy a walk is a superfluous addition to a hiking guide. I beg to differ, however, because this prominent point offers one of the finest unobstructed views in Santa Barbara County. From this lookout you can see down onto the beautiful Santa Barbara coastline stretching from Refugio Beach all the way to Point Mugu. Out to sea you can see the islands dotting the Santa Barbara Channel looking like huge migrating whales in some Disney fantasy gone awry. To the north you'll gaze into the rugged heart of the Santa Barbara Backcountry, into the un-sullied canyons of the San Rafael and Dick Smith wilderness areas. High peaks dominate here: Santa Cruz, Big Pine, Madulce. Lake Cachuma and Gibraltar reservoirs glisten blue in the canyons below. If you're a newcomer to this backcountry, by all means make this one of your first stops. Bring along a picnic lunch and a good map and plan for a thoroughly enjoyable lesson in the regions's geography.

Driving: La Cumbre Roadhead.

Directions: From the locked gate on East Camino Cielo, walk up the paved road until it forks. Follow either fork to a soon to be removed fire lookout. There are picnic tables under the pines.
TOPO: *Santa Barbara*

#7
KNAPP'S LODGE
1 Mile Round Trip

Description: By 1890, the social structure of Santa Barbara County was clearly changing. Before then, the population consisted largely of Spaniards from the rancho era, Anglo homesteaders, and dispirited prospectors who had drifted south from the gold fields. As the century mark approached, however, an increasing number of wealthy retirees, attracted by the fine climate, spectacular setting, and magazine articles extolling these virtures, began to call Santa Barbara their home.

One member of this new migration was George Owen Knapp, former chairman of the Union Carbide Corporation, who arrived on the scene in 1912. Knapp was a man of unusual energy who had risen from the bottom of his field to the top of his profession. He was a civic-minded individual, and he loved to build things, contributing generously to the construction of schools, churches, and hospitals for the growing community. He also liked building roads and is largely responsible for the construction of the ridgetop Camino Cielo Road along the summit of the Santa Ynez Range.

In 1916, Knapp purchased a 160-acre tract near the top of the Santa Ynez Mountains and set out to build himself a home. And what a home it was. It took 20 men over four years to construct the five-bedroom mansion. It featured a massive dining room, servants' quarters for six, a separate groundskeeper's house, and even Knapp's own private observatory, all set on a bluff high above the Santa Ynez River Canyon. Not to be stopped here, Knapp built a road from his property to the foot of Wellhouse Falls in Lewis Canyon below his home. There he put in a pumphouse and an observation deck. He installed a system of locks and pumps in Lewis Creek so that water could be impounded upstream. On cue the locks would open allowing a torrent to rush over the falls in a silvery cascade. To highlight the effect, spotlights were installed to illuminate the falls at night. And, lest his guests lack entertainment, a speaker system was installed and live organ music piped down from the house.

Knapp lived much of the rest of his long and happy life at his lodge in the sky. But in 1940, shortly after the property changed hands, the mansion was destroyed in the Paradise Canyon Fire. The observatory remained intact on the site for many years but met a similar fate in the 1964 Coyote Fire. Today, the fireplace and foundation ruins are all that remain of the grand estate. But hikers can still enjoy the magnificent view of the Santa Barbara Backcountry from this site. One can sit here and gaze for miles out over the nearby wilderness thinking back to a time when life was a bit more simple. And a bit more elegant.

Driving: Snyder Roadhead.

Directions: Walk north past the locked gate onto the fire road, which is the Snyder trail (28W02). In a short while you round a bend and climb the remaining short distance up to the ruins of Knapp's Lodge. Enjoy the ruins, poke among the old fireplaces, and imagine what a magnificent mansion this must once have been.

When it's time to go, retrace your steps back to East Camino Cielo. **TOPO:** *San Marcos Pass*

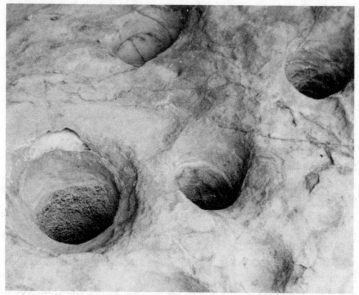

Because Chumash Indian squaws ground acorns into meal at the same backcountry campsites each year, mortar holes gradually developed in the sandstone.

#8
THE ALISO CANYON NATURE TRAIL
3 Mile Loop

Description: If you're a newcomer to the Santa Barbara Backcountry, one of the better ways to acquaint you with some of its natural splendors is to sample the Aliso Canyon Nature Trail in lower Santa Ynez Canyon. This loop trip begins at Sage Hill Group Campground and climbs up Aliso Canyon to a viewpoint on a ridge high above the Santa Ynez before returning back to the camp. At one point your route will intersect the trail to Upper Oso Campground and you can continue hiking up Oso Creek in that direction should you wish to extend your walk. The text for the nature trail was prepared by the 11- to 14-year-old students from the Santa Barbara Open Alternative School who spent the Spring of 1982 exploring and studying the environment here. The concept and text for the trail are all a product of their work. Since the brochure for the trail is often not available, the students' text is reprinted below.

Driving: Sage Hill Roadhead.

Directions: Follow the wide trail into Aliso Canyon to:

Signpost No. 1: This rock formation of Monterey Shale was formed as layers of sediment in a broad ocean base about 20 million years ago. About a million years ago the sedimentary beds were compressed, folded, and faulted as the North American continent pushed against the tectonic plates in the Pacific Ocean. As you walk along the trail, you can see sandstone and shale which show signs of folding and faulting such as the drag marks you see here.

Signpost No. 2: Oak Woodland Community. As you can see, the trees are mainly the coast live oak. It has evergreen holly-like leaves. The Chumash Indians used the acorns as a food source. Those funny round things on the oak tree are oak galls. The gall wasp makes them and uses them as a place to put its eggs. In the spring the grass is full of wildflowers and, if you listen carefully, you might hear the black-and-white acorn woodpecker making holes in the trees to store his food. If you walk quietly, you might see a ground squirrel, a brush rabbit, or a striped skunk. You might hear the sound of a California valley quail, a short, plump bird who lives throughout the chaparrel. Its plume extends forward, which differentiates it from the straight plume of the mountain quail.

Signpost No. 3: If you look across the creekbed you will see a very large toyon or California holly. The roots of the toyon are holding up the sides of the creek. It has red berries at Christmas, white flowers, and green, sharp-toothed leaves. The Chumash Indians made tea from the bark and used the leaves to cure aches and pains. (Unfortunately, this toyon recently expired. However, you will find other examples of the species farther up the canyon.)

Signpost No. 4: Do you see a tree nearby that looks different? It's the one with the white-and-gray, blotchy bark. It's called a sycamore or *aliso* tree. It grows by the water and during the summer when the creek drys up there's enough water stored underground so it won't die. Along this small meadow you'll probably see some butterflies such as the monarch, swallowtail, or buckeye. Can you see the holes in the ground where the pocket gopher lives? These rodents have a short blunt nose and dig everywhere. (Stay left at the trail junction up ahead.)

Signpost No. 5: Riparian Community. Now you will notice the unmistakable smell of a riparian area. Plants like mosses, willows, reeds, rushes, and stream orchids grow here. Animal tracks in the mud show that many species come here for water such as the raccoon. You might also see the racer, a small dark snake with yellow side stripes. It lives by the water most of the time, but it is also found in the grassy areas near rocks. Mosquitoes, flies, butterflies, and ladybugs are usually seen. The water comes alive with the dancing of the waterstrider insect. As you walk along, look for the blacktailed deer. If you are really quiet, you might see one drinking at the creek or eating sagebrush or mistletoe.

Signpost No. 6: The Chumash Indians used poison oak leaves as a cure for warts, and the berries to dye their baskets. It has shiny toothed leaves in clusters of three. At some times of the year they are red. Deer eat the leaves, and birds and rodents eat the white berries. Look around and you will see mugwort, which, when crushed and rubbed on the skin, may keep you from getting poison oak. It has long slender leaves that are silvery underneath.

Signpost No. 7: Stop and enjoy yourself here. Sit down and listen to the birds and insects. Look at the trees, flowers, and rocks. This is a place for you to be quiet and become aware of all the animals and plants in this wild canyon. If you see a bird that looks like a pigeon, it's probably a dove. If you hear a "coo-o-coo-coo-coo," it's the mourning dove.

Signpost No. 8: You will notice a change as you walk into the dry brush areas away from the creek. In the spring two bulb plants bloom. Both were used by the Indians for food: The purple brodeia and the Mariposa lily. The lily is shaped like the California poppy but has three petals. As the area opens up you may see some reptiles like the king snake. It has smooth shiny plates and is black with creamy stripes around its body. It eats rodents, small birds, and bird eggs. You may also see an earth-colored rattlesnake, the only poisonous snake in California. It often gives warning before striking. A red-tailed hawk might be soaring above you. It has a darkish head, a brown-and-white body, and a red tail. It can sit in one place for hours and then suddenly swoop down to catch a reptile or small animal.

Signpost No. 9: Sapsucker Oak Tree. See the holes on the right side of this tree? The yellow-bellied sapsucker made them. They drill these holes so they can get sap and insects to eat. Insects sometimes use these holes for homes.

Signpost No.10: Many different kinds of lupine grow all over the California hillsides. In spring, yellow and purple lupine grow here along with golden yarrow and red and yellow Indian paintbrush. You can identify lupine by its unusual palm-shaped leaf and upright flower stalk.

Signpost No. 11: Chaparral Community. You are walking through the chaparral, a very thick shrubby growth that makes an ideal shelter for birds and animals. Chamise is the plant you see with the spiney leaves. There is also a lot of yerba santa, which the Indians boiled and used for a variety of cures. Blue- or white-flowered ceonothus is very fragrant when you brush up against it in the springtime. If you look down the creek toward the Santa Ynez Mountain Range, you will see how thick the chaparral can grow.

Signpost No. 12: Smell the leaves of the white sage. The Indians used them as a hair wash, a drink, and in ceremonies. As you are walking the trail, look for other sage plants. They all have a distinctive spike-like flower arrangement.

Signpost No. 13: Looking down the creekbed, you can see the dark, rounded lava pillows of Franciscan shale formed during the Jurrassic period. This shows us that there was once volcanic activity in this area.

Signpost No. 14: If you climb the shale slope, you will see unusual plants that are able to survive in this harsh environment. As you climb the hill, take your time. See if you can identify any of the plants you have learned; listen for the sounds that the insects make; look at how the plants change as you climb higher. In the spring count how many different types of wildflowers you can find. You may see coreopsis, clarkia, chia, monkey flower, California poppy, and the spikey yucca. It takes years for the yucca to reach blooming size. The Chumash used it to make sandals, baskets, and cords.

(You have now hiked one mile and the trail will leave Aliso Canyon to climb up to the top of the ridge. The climb is steep but the views are worth it. The next stop is about ⅓ mile up the hill.)

Signpost No. 15: In the spring look for a group of soaproot plants with long curly leaves close to the ground. By fall only the long thin stalks will remain. The Chumash used the other bulb fibers to make brushes. The inner bulb was cooked and pressed into flat cakes and dried for food. The raw bulbs were mashed and used as soap or put in the water to stun fish so they could be caught more easily.

Signpost No. 16: As you continue up the meadow notice the edge of the thick chaparral, especially the large clumps of grayish-purple sage. In the spring these grassy meadows or potreros have many wildflowers such as purple nightshade, peony, blue-eyed grass, popcorn flower, woolie blue curls, and the California poppy.

Signpost No. 17: The hilltop is a great place for watching birds because the winds help them soar. You might be lucky to see a California condor, a large vulture. It's the biggest bird in North America with a wing span of about nine feet. There are fewer than 30 of them left in California. You might also see the rare golden eagle, which is about three-and-a-half feet long with a wing span of up to eight feet. You could also look for the turkey vulture, which can look like a hawk soaring in the sky except it tips from side to side to adjust its eyesight. The vulture eats meat, but because it has no sharp talons it has to eat the leftovers of other animals.

Signpost No. 18: At this highest point of the nature trail, the Santa Ynez Range is to the south and the San Rafael Range is to the north. The range to the north is of Matilija sandstone from the Eocene Epoch. The Little Pine Fault runs through this area. This is a good spot to rest. Pick a rock to sit down on, look around at the view, and feel the energy of the wind.

Signpost No. 19: You are standing on a hillside formed by the carving action of the Santa Ynez River. The river provides food for shore birds, fish, and insects. Watch for the flight of the great blue heron along the river.

Signpost No. 20: In 1980 there was a prescribed burn in this area. Soon there was new plant growth from the underground burls, which is the way the chaparral plants recover. You will see morning glory and deerweed everywhere. You may also see some flowers that seem out of place growing here. They were planted to help stabilize the soil when the area was seeded after the trail was built.

Signpost No. 21: Close to the ground you see the chia sage. California Indians put a seed under each eyelid to reduce swelling. They also ate a handful before any long march for energy. Notice the gray-leafed purple sage nearby. Its lavender, mintlike flowers make the slopes look a soft purple color from a distance.

Continue down the grassy slope to a junction with the Aliso Trail. Turn left here and hike the rest of the way back to the car.

TOPO: *San Marcos Pass*

THE SWIMMING HOLES
GIBRALTAR DAM
Loop

Description: Long one of my favorite day hikes in the Los Padres, I try to enjoy this walk whenever I'm car camping with friends in the Paradise area. Unfortunately, this pool-studded portion of the Santa Ynez River is hardly a secret, and it's particularly popular with young people from Santa Barbara. So popular in fact that, several years ago, the Forest Service closed the trail camp at the foot of the dam to control a serious pollution problem. But don't be deterred. By following my high route to the dam you'll be able to scout out many of the more secluded pools in the river from above which are not apparent to hikers on the canyon floor. Pick out one or several that interest you, then explore them on your way back out.

Driving: Redrock Roadhead.

Directions: From the parking area, scout out Fire Road 5N18 to the southeast and head uphill. The road quickly gains 200 feet and then levels off, contouring high above the Santa Ynez. Continue on easily until you catch site of the imposing face of Gibraltar Dam 2.5 miles from the start. The reservoir, named for the large rock here that has an uncanny resemblance to its Mediterranean cousin, was built in 1920 and impounds drinking water for Santa Barbara. Trespassing on the dam is strictly forbidden, so descend on the fire road to its foot. Here you'll find an especially large swimming hole and, just downstream, what remains of Gibraltar Trail Camp. When I last visited here there were two stoves and tables provided for day use. It's a good spot for a picnic.

When it's time to continue, hike downstream along the Santa Ynez. Just below the dam, you'll pass the ruins of an old quicksilver mine dating back to the turn of the century. Numerous swimming holes abound along the river and, if you've picked out your special spot earlier, now is the time to explore.

When it's time to continue, leisurely follow the riverbed back to the car.

TOPO: *Little Pine Mountain*

A mystic pictograph, perhaps depicting the sun as the source of all life and power, at an ancient Chumash Indian campsite.

#10
NOJOQUI FALLS COUNTY PARK
0.6 Miles Round Trip

Description: Tucked into a cool rural canyon on the north slope of the Santa Ynez Mountains is one of Santa Barbara County's more attractive parks, where you can picnic, play, or take the kids on a pleasant hike they won't soon forget. The going is easy, the path well marked and scented with the fragrance of bay.

Driving: Nojoqui Roadhead.

Directions: From the end of the parking lot, follow the wide trail up the cool forested canyon along the all-year creek. After crossing a wooden bridge, your efforts are soon rewarded by your first view of streaming Nojoqui Falls. Follow the trail a short distance to the grotto at its foot. Return the way you came.

TOPO: *Solvang*

#11
GAVIOTA HOT SPRINGS
1 Mile Round Trip

Description: Although technically part of Gaviota State Park, this trip merits inclusion in this volume because it takes the hiker to one of the more interesting parts of the Santa Barbara Backcountry. "Hot springs" is something of a misnomer; "tepid" would be more accurate since the water here maintains an average temperature of 75 degrees Fahrenheit. A dip in the pleasant pool is nonetheless an enjoyable experience, and after a half-hour soak, I guarantee you'll feel at least some cares drift away. One word of caution: Skinnydipping, though tempting, is officially forbidden, and park rangers do patrol the area.

Driving: Gaviota Roadhead.

Directions: From the parking area, walk up the wide dirt road a moderate 0.5 mile under a canopy of live oaks to the spring. When you've enjoyed your soak, return the same way.

TOPO: *Solvang*

#12
A DAY TRIP TO POOL ROCK
AND CONDOR CAVE
5 Miles Round Trip

Description: Over my years of hiking I've found many exceptional places in the Santa Barbara Backcountry. Certainly among my favorites are the Seven Falls of Mission Canyon, the cascades of Devil's Gate, and Montgomery Portero when the wildflowers are in bloom. These are so special because man has left them alone, coming to visit and then just going away. But there are other equally uncommon places in this backcountry that are special because man has changed them. I'm not referring to those altered by our high-tech society, but to places which were sacred to and used by the ancient Chumash Indians. That these were ceremonial sites is well established. But the rituals that were performed here, the meaning behind the mysterious pictographs, these are long shrouded in the past. There is an aura at these places, a feeling of some subtle kind of magic. On this trip I'll take you to two such Chumash shrines.

Driving: NIRA Roadhead.

Directions: Follow the Manzana Trail (30W13) upstream into the San Rafael Wilderness for an easy mile to a junction at Lost Valley Camp. Turn left here onto the Lost Valley Trail (20W14), which is really an old Jeep road for much of its length dating back to Civilian Conservation Corps days. The trail ascends to the top of an old stream terrace in 0.7 miles and then turns north. In less than a mile your route passes through a washout near a chimney of rock and continues upstream. Two miles beyond Lost Valley Camp, the canyon opens up and a large side canyon flows in from the northwest. Head up this side canyon, following the faint trail near the streambed. In 0.1 miles there's a canyon junction, stay right. A quarter-mile farther on the canyon narrows and comes to another canyon junction. Make a note of it because you'll be returning to it later, but at this point turn to the right and continue upstream. In less than half a mile where there's a large rock on the side of the canyon wall your route turns to the north. Shortly thereafter, just as you pass a small canyon coming in from the west, you'll note a faint foot trail climbing the steep shale ridge that separates the two canyons. Follow it up along the narrow part of the ridge as it enters the chaparral on the flat plateau between these two canyons. You can see Pool Rock through the brush to the north. A short distance on, passing around the east side of a large rock, you will reach the Indian caves near the northeast corner of the rock. Then following along the north side you will come to a lower area that has footholds chipped into the rock. This is the Indian Trail to the pool at the top of Pool Rock.

To reach the Condor Cave retrace your steps back downstream to the aforementioned junction. Turn right and continue 0.3 miles upstream to the cave located in a large sandstone outcropping just west of the creek. You will notice a hole caused by wind erosion in the east end of the cave and a pictograph of a large condor notable for the red-shaded head painted on the face of the cave.

When it's time to go, retrace your steps back down the canyon to Manzana Creek and continue on to the roadhead.

TOPO: *Bald Mountain.* W/A

#13
TO THE TOP OF NORDHOFF'S PEAK
12 Miles Round Trip

Description: In 1872, journalist Charles Nordhoff, while on his second visit to Southern California, heard tale that just 15 miles inland from the sleepy mission town of San Buenaventura was a lush beautiful valley with all-year streams, crystal clean air, and several natural hot springs. Nordhoff rented a horse, rode up the Ventura River, and discovered for himself the beautiful valley of Ojai. Returning to New York, he published numerous articles, including one in the prestigious *Harper's Magazine,* extolling the many health benefits of this valley. And it wasn't long before wealthy easterners were making vacation pilgrimages to visit this Shangri-la. In fact, they came in droves.

The town that grew in the valley (as well as the nearby peak) was named for the author who had popularized it, and the hamlet thrived. Although the city fathers eventually adopted the name Ojai, meaning "nest," in the early 1900s, Nordhoff's name is still attached to the 4,425-foot peak that dominates the valley. The summit of that peak, with its spectacular views of the Ventura County backcountry, is the subject of this hike.

Driving: Gridley Roadhead.

Description: Your trek begins at the end of the Gridley Road where a sign directs you onto the recently reworked route of the Gridley Trail (22W05). You climb up the moderately steep pathway shaded by thick laurel sumac and other hardy brush a cool half-mile to the Gridley Fire Road (5N11). Turn right here. As you hike along this well-graded and retiring old roadway, you pass along the perimeter of some newly planted avocado groves. These orchards utilize a technique called "drip irrigation," which is revolutionizing agriculture in this arid part of the state. The tiny holes punched in the black hoses that lace the mountainside allow water and nutrients to be applied slowly and directly to the roots of the growing plants. This lets them thrive on hillsides as steep as 45 degrees.

You pass a small apiary, bear left at a junction, and travel beyond the thriving groves into Gridley Canyon. Soon you hear Gridley Creek cascading far below. At the same time, notice the nearly vertical ribbed rock striations on Peak 2968 and its lower sister summit, evidence of the violent earthmoving processes that created these mountains. Continuing uphill, your route turns to the northwest and the trail hugs the cooler, moister side of the canyon where berry-laden toyon and pink phlox thrive in season. If you lift your gaze skyward at this point, you can see all the way to the fire lookout marking the summit as Nordhoff Peak. Soon thereafter you reach what's left of the little trail camp at Gridley Spring. In 1985, the holocaust that was the Wheeler Fire badly damaged the mountainside in this area, and the trail camp was one of the victims of those flames. A reliable spring remains as well as a single stove.

From Gridley Spring, continue along the dirt road for a half-mile to cross a tributary stream. A trail then begins switchbacking along a ridgeback to the top of the Topatopas to meet the Nordhoff Fire Road (5N05) in 2 miles. Turn left here and follow this road to the top of Nordhoff Peak, 1 more mile.

Tiresome as this climb is, the views are well worth it. To the south, the verdant Ojai Valley is spread out beneath your feet and you can see out to the Channel Islands and the Pacific Ocean on a clear day. You can hardly fail to notice the gleaming blue jewel of Lake Casitas, a recreational reservoir in the foothills. To the northeast and west, you can study over half a million acres of the Los Padres National Forest, sighting the high mountains of the San Rafael and Dick Smith wilderness areas as well as the nearby slopes of the Sespe Condor Sanctuary. All in all, the lookout on Nordhoff Peak is a superb place from which to gain a richer perspective of the geography of this corner of the state. One word of caution though: In winter, snow will often cover the higher elevations of this climb and make it difficult if not downright hazardous.

When it's time to leave, return the way you came.

TOPOS: *Ojai, Lion Canyon*

#14
A DAYHIKE UP TO SANTA PAULA PEAK
9 Miles Round Trip

Description: With an elevation of 4,957 feet, Santa Paula Peak is certainly not the highest point in Ventura County. But the views from the top are nevertheless impressive and the hike to it quite a challenge. From the summit, you can see the miles upon miles of neatly laid out orchards carpeting the lush Santa Clara Valley, one of the major citrus producing regions of Southern California. You have views out to the faraway Channel Islands and into the rugged country of the Sespe Condor Sanctuary. Once on top, you might just enjoy that peaceful feeling that comes after a good workout and let the reliable onshore breeze cool you down. For reasons that will be obvious after you do this trip, Santa Paula Peak has long been used by local Sierra Club chapters as an early season conditioning hike. Be sure to pack along plenty of cool water and a lunch.

Driving: Timber Canyon Roadhead.

Directions: Walk onto the Santa Paul Peak Trail (20W16) and almost immediately begin your moderate ascent. The trail soon climbs over to a ridgeback and climbs steeply through the heavy chaparral. There are more than a dozen switchbacks on the way to the top and I guarantee your rest stops will be many. After more than 4 miles of hearty climbing, you reach the ridge just below the summit, bear to the west, and walk the remaining distance to the top. The Sierra Club's 100 Peaks Section maintains a summit register here.

When it's time to go, retrace your steps.

TOPO: *Santa Paula Peak.* F/C

#15
ROSE VALLEY FALLS
0.5 Miles Round Trip

Description: Offering fishing and swimming in three adjacent artificial lakes as well as access to nearby Sespe Creek, it's no wonder that Rose Valley Campground has long been a popular destination for car campers. Yet another happy adjunct to a weekend at Rose Valley is the hike up to one of the most beautiful waterfalls in Southern California. Dropping in two tiers from a height of over 300 feet, the falls provide a bridal veil of beauty against the steep forested slope. On this trip you'll hike to the foot of the lower fall where there is a cool fern-dotted grotto.

Driving: Rose Valley Roadhead.

Directions: The trail begins near campsite No. 4, heads into the woods, and quickly crosses the stream. After a couple more crossings you find yourself hiking up a cool north-facing canyon where the scent of bay tinges the air. You'll notice some trails to the left made by use which tumble down to Rose Creek to its dozen of small falls, cascades, and pools. Less than a third of a mile from the campground, you reach the foot of the spectacular 100-foot lower fall where you can just sit and enjoy the music.

Although it's possible for a skilled scrambler to reach the upper fall, the way is treacherous and I recommend against it. There have been repeated bad accidents among those who have tried.

When it's time to go retrace your steps.

TOPO: *Lion Canyon*

#16
A CLIMB TO McPHERSON LOOKOUT
10 Mile Loop

Description: This was by far the day excursion I enjoyed most during my scouting for this guide. The route travels from deeply shaded Aliso Park Campground to a fire lookout atop 5,747-foot McPherson Peak and returns on a little-used trail down the backbone of a ridge to complete a 10-mile loop. For my hike I chose a clear windy day in late February about two weeks after a light snowfall had dusted the ridges of the Sierra Madres. The dazzling whiteness of the McPherson summit presented a glistening contrast between the chaparral-shrouded San Rafael Wilderness to the southwest, the open and colorful Cuyama Badlands below, and a distant expanse of the southern Sierra Nevada to the northeast. I guarantee a spectacular outing to any hiker blessed with such a day.

Driving: Aliso Roadhead.

Directions: From Aliso Park, walk up the jeep road that leaves camp and travel through chaparral to Hog Pen Spring Camp in 2.2 miles. This camp was named by the McPhersons, a family of ranchers that long ago raised hogs here at the spring. Water is available from a faucet.

Continue southwest on Trail 27W01, which takes off from the camp, and climb and switchback your way moderately up a yucca-studded chaparral slope to reach the Sierra Madre Road (32S13) in 1.8 miles. Turn right here (north) and follow the road until you see the lookout tower on McPherson Peak ahead. You may continue easily along the road, which has impressive views to both sides (bear right at an intersection to reach the peak in 2 miles) or cut off crosscountry and save yourself half a mile.

Once on the summit, stop for lunch and rest to experience the great joy of being on high places. When you are ready to leave, scout around to the east below the lookout for the Old McPherson Trail (27W02). It's not hard to find. Follow it down along a ridge of the peak through chaparral. It reaches an indistinct junction with an abandoned trail in 2 miles where you should bear right. Then continue moderately downhill and back to Aliso Park in another 2 miles, taking your time to enjoy the ever changing views of the Cuyama Valley. Should you wish to spend the night in the oak-shaded surroundings of Aliso Campground, supplies are available in nearby New Cuyama.

TOPO: *Peak Mountain*

Chaparral carpets the hillsides along the Agua Blanca Trail north of Lake Piru.

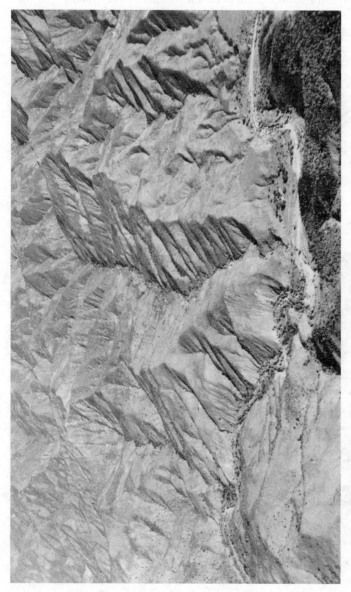

Sisquoc River near Wellman Canyon in the San Rafael Wilderness. (U.S. FOREST SERVICE)

IV

EASY OVERNIGHT BACKPACK TRIPS IN THE SOUTHERN LOS PADRES

I know that many of you reading this guide are bound by duty and commitment, as I often am, to an occupation that keeps you in the city five days a week. With only an occasional weekend to get out on the trails, you're looking for places you can trek to in a day for an easy overnight campout "to get away from it all." Some of you are also looking for an easy trip to introduce a friend or family member to the joys of backpacking. You don't want to go on a marathon journey and discourage your companion.

For all of you with these requirements, I've listed in this section my favorite short overnight backpack destinations in the Santa Barbara Backcountry. The following trip suggestions describe trail camps you can walk to easily in one day. Here you can enjoy a peaceful backcountry night at the camp that is the destination of each hike. There are camp stoves at each site and reliable water from January through early May. The following is an alphabetical list of those camps. With each camp is the TOTAL ROUND TRIP walking distance, that is, from the roadhead to the camp and back to the roadhead. In all cases, you'll return along the same trail you took in. The driving directions to each roadhead, a listing of facilities and topo maps needed, will be found in the Trail Camps and Roadheads chapters of this guide.

#17
BEARTRAP
10 Miles Round Trip

It may seem hard to believe today, but until the early 1900s grizzly bears were a serious menace to travelers in our mountains. This particular trip will take you two canyons away from civilization to a camp named for the trapping activities of the Reyes family, who long ago ran cattle out in the Cuyama Valley. You'll be surprised by the reliable creek that runs through camp here on the desert side of the Los Padres Forest. You will find this destination quiet and shaded by Douglas fir, sugar pine, incense cedar, and ponderosa pine trees. Snow sometimes visits at this elevation (5,000 feet) in winter.

#18
CEDAR CREEK
6.2 Miles Round Trip

Incense cedars, Jeffrey and sugar pines at this campsite might conjure up visions of a trip through the Sierra Nevada. But right here in the Santa Barbara Backcountry at the 5,000-foot level these trees thrive in the cool environment of an tributary of Piru Creek. The trip in involves little elevation gain and water can be counted upon virtually all year. Goldhounds will sometimes be encountered along the Piru panning for the sparkling metal. Little ones should not be tired by the easy trek.

#19
CHORRO GRANDE SPRING
2 Miles Round Trip

Even neophytes to backpacking will not be intimidated by the easy hike to this little camp. You merely follow the trail an easy mile down from the top of Pine Mountain to this site shaded by pines, live oaks, and a smattering of white fir near a most reliable stream. The views out over the headwaters of Sespe Creek at sunset are memorable. You will most likely find snow here in winter.

#20
FORBUSH FLAT
3.4 Miles Round Trip

If you live in Santa Barbara, leave work a little early on Friday and spend the weekend up at Forbush Flat. Located on the edge of a potrero where Fred Forbush built his cabin in 1910, the camp has room for up to four parties of hikers. Explore a little bit and you'll find the remains of an orchard planted by Forbush more than three-quarters of a century ago. At 2,000 feet, the camp is open all year.

#21
HADDOCK
11.6 Miles Round Trip

To reach Haddock, you hike along the forested ridge of Pine Mountain nearly the entire way and enjoy magnificant views in all directions. Haddock is something of a crossroads camp on Pine Mountain and is often used by the Boy Scouts. But since the sites here are quite spread out, there's room for a number of people. You can use Haddock as a weekend base camp and dayhike into the drainages of Reyes and Piedra Blanca Creek from here. There is snow in winter.

#22
MATILIJA
2 Miles Round Trip

Although this camp has repeatedly suffered fire and flood damage over the past 20 years, the Forest Service continues to restore it. The hike in could only be described as easy; expect, however, to get your feet wet in rushing Matilija Creek. Visitors usually find the pattern of stream erosion on the canyon walls here fascinating.

#23
MIDDLE CALIENTE
2 Miles Round Trip

After years of disuse, this camp was recently restored to a serviceable condition through volunteer effort. The hike in is quite easy, the camp comfortable to visit, and water generally reliable except in the peak of summer. There is a large swimming hole downstream from the camp and I have been told of a high waterfall about 2½ miles upstream. After a visit to Middle Caliente, you can enjoy a soothing soak in the natural hot springs located near the roadhead.

#24
MIDDLE MATILIJA
6.2 Miles Round Trip

Like its sister camp downstream, Middle Mitilija has repeatedly been damaged by fire and storm. It is, however, in serviceable condition. The hike to the camp is uphill, primarily on a retiring jeep road. The area is shaded by oaks and the creek generally reliable.

#25
MURIETTA
2 Miles Round Trip

Named for the either legendary or apocraphyl Mexican badman, Joaquin Murietta, this little camp is one of my favorite destinations near Ojai. The hike in is quite easy and the camp a delight to visit. It's located on a small flat shaded by hefty live oaks. Unfortunately, the camp is also a favorite of local Boy Scouts, so be prepared for some weekend company.

#26
POTRERO JOHN
3.2 Miles Round Trip

In English we'd call this camp John's Meadow. It was named after John Power, an early landowner in this portion of the Sespe country who grazed his horses in the area. Potrero John is rarely visited as the trail beyond camp goes nowhere. The canyon is very quiet and you probably won't be bothered here by anybody else. Stream water is, however, intermittent and often ceases to flow during the hot summers.

#27
SHEEP
10 Miles Round Trip

If you're extraordinarily fortunate you might sight a soaring condor during this hike down from Mt. Piños. The camp is set in a shallow pine-forested canyon on the North Fork Trail. Wild lilies grow near-by. Water may be obtained from a spring about a quarter mile above the camp. With an elevation of 8,200 feet, this site makes for a good conditioning hike before heading off to the High Sierra. Expect quite a bit of snow in winter.

#28
TWIN FORKS
4.8 Miles Round Trip

This camp in the Sespe drainage is on a small grassy flat above the confluence of the Twin Forks of Piedra Blanca Creek. If you enjoy being lulled to sleep by the cascading music of falling water, you will definitely find this to be a peaceful place. There are some small swimming holes above the camp on the middle fork of the creek. Should all the sites be taken, an alternative just a short distance down the trail is Piedra Blanca Camp.

#29
UPPER RANCHO NUEVO
9.6 Miles Round Trip

In the late 1830s, partly due to drought and also due to a land dispute with the padres at San Fernando Mission, the Reyes family of Encino drove their livestock out of the San Fernando Valley and up over the Grapevine into the Cuyama Valley of Santa Barbara County. At that time this portion of the Southland was a complete wilderness, and so it was here that the Reyes family set up their new household. Among the areas they named was Rancho Nuevo, which means "new ranch." Upper Rancho Nuevo is located up the creek by the same name at the end of the trail. It's not suitable for summer visits because of the extreme heat. However, in wintertime the temperatures are cool, stream water is reliable, and the surrounding peaks are covered by snow.

#30
UPPER REYES
7 Miles Round Trip

Because of the rushing creek here on the desert side of the mountains, the shaded location, and good fishing possibilities, this camp makes for a fine weekend retreat. I have only rarely encountered any other hikers in the vicinity. An ideal arrangement would be to arrive Friday night at the roadhead, where there is an attractive car campground, hike in Saturday, hike out Sunday, and, before leaving, enjoy a cook drink at nearby Scheideck's Camp on the patio that hangs out over the bubbling stream.

#31
McGUIRE
2.6 Miles Round Trip

Although Pine Mountain is a favorite springtime camping destination for many people, few seem to come to this little camp on the mountain's north slope. Here at the site of a hunting camp established long ago by old man McGuire, a rancher from Ojai, you can watch hawks, eagles, maybe even a condor soar on the thermal air currents and enjoy beautiful views to the north. You'll also find a reliable spring right in camp. There is snow in winter.

#32
THE PINES
6 Miles Round Trip

Experimental forests to test the hardiness of different pine species in Southern California's hostile environment were quite an innovation in the early 1900s. And one of the first forests of this type was planted on this little flat high above the Ojai Valley. Subsequent fires have destroyed the original seedlings but over the years they have been replanted. The hike up to this spot is moderate but the views thoroughly enjoyable. There is a reliable spring near camp.

A lone hiker explores the beautiful Madulce Trail in the Dick Smith Wilderness. (U.S. FOREST SERVICE)

V

SHUTTLE AND LOOP TRIPS THROUGH THE SANTA BARBARA BACKCOUNTRY

In the preceding chapter, I've described some easy overnight backpack trips where you return from your backcountry destination by retracing your steps along the same trail you took in. This next set of trip suggestions, however, will take you on more complex journeys. What I offer you are a series of shuttle (where you begin and end at different roadheads, thus necessitating a car shuttle) and loop trips (where you travel in a circle and return to the same roadhead). These are generally longer treks than the ones I have described so far. Some take as long as a week to complete and involve the use of several trail camps. Some will take you into the primitive outback of Ventura County and many travel through the San Rafael or Dick Smith wilderness areas. They all explore what I consider to be the most scenic and beautiful portions of the Santa Barbara Backcountry.

Some of these hikes are rough and difficult and definitely not for the neophyte. Some backcountry experience is necessary; routefinding expertise, essential. You will often be many miles from the nearest road, so proper provisioning will be important. Refer to the "Backcountry Travelers' Checklist" at the end of this volume (page 173) when preparing for your trip to be sure you don't leave any essential article behind. You might also augment your wilderness skills by reviewing one of the many fine books on the subject. *Backpacking: One Step at a Time* by Harvey Manning is especially thorough and up to date.

In the following pages I'll provide you with 23 trips through the Santa Barbara Backcountry. In each case I'll give you total round-trip mileage, complete hiking directions from beginning to end, historical notes that seem pertinent, and a list of topographic maps to bring along.

Directions to the roadheads can be found by consulting the ''Road-heads'' chapter which begins on page 155. Complete information on each trail camp, its size, facilities, and water availability, can be found in the ''Trail Camps'' chapter which begins on page 107. Geographically, the trips are listed starting from the Los Angeles/Ventura county line and progressing west and then north. As elsewhere in this volume, the notation ''F/C'' means that that particular trip falls into the traditional summer fire closure. Likewise, ''W/A'' means you will be hiking and camping in a wilderness area.

With eyesight eight times sharper than man's, the Red Tail Hawk is frequently seen soaring high above the Santa Barbara Backcountry in search of prey. (U.S. FOREST SERVICE)

#33
INTO THE AGUA BLANCA COUNTRY
ABOVE LAKE PIRU
10.4 Mile Loop

Description: I have long been partial to this weekend backpacking route for its variety of experiences: quiet canyon, cool forest, rolling grassy meadow. The solitude is also inviting. You will meet few hikers back in this corner of the Los Padres north of Lake Piru. On this varied springtime backpack, you'll travel into the secluded canyon of the Agua Blanca and then return by a high trail through a geological sink and across an expansive hillside pasture. This is a fine overnight trip for a group in good condition.

Driving: Blue Point Roadhead.

Directions: Walk north from the campground along sandy Piru Creek on an old dirt road toward Kester's Camp. Then bear left up Agua Blanca Creek on the Agua Blanca Trail (19W10). The trail is washed out in sections and your progress will be reasonably slow during the 4.5-mile trek to Log Cabin Camp, your overnight destination. It's located just beyond Devil's Gateway, and you must either ford the creek at this narrows or follow a short steep trail up and around this point to reach the shady camp.

Your return route follows the Pothole Trail (18W04), which takes off just downstream from the camp and climbs steeply up the south canyon wall. There is a lot of poison oak. Your ascent levels off in 1 mile as you pass a private cabin near a marshy spot where there is a deep forest and travel onto the Devil's Potrero and the Pothole, a geological depression caused by the shifting of underground faults in the area. You next climb up the slope above the Pothole through chaparral, and there are excellent views here back down to Agua Blanca Creek. The trail continues for 3.4 miles on an easy ascent and then drops down along the backbone of a ridge via a firebreak. The Pothole Trail finally peters out about halfway down the grassy slope, where you will find cattle grazing, but with Lake Piru and the Blue Point Road clearly in view, you can easily plan your descent to the road

The California quail, the state bird, is one of many wild inhabitants of the Santa Barbara Backcountry. (U.S. FOREST SERVICE)

you followed when you first drove into the campground. Simply continue 1 mile crosscountry down the slope to the road; when you reach it, turn left and walk the remaining distance (less than 0.5 miles) to the campground and your car. This is overall a moderately strenuous hike.

TOPO: *Cobblestone Mountain.* F/C

#34
A DIFFICULT BACKPACK DOWN AGUA BLANCA CREEK
19.4 Miles One Way

Description: Since much of this route is washed out or overgrown, and some distances are traveled in a trailless streambed where wading is necessary, this three-day hike is for hardy, experienced backpackers *only.* The rewards are ample, however, for the area is wild and beautiful. Plan to spend your nights at Ant and Cove Camps.

Driving: Start at Dough Flat Roadhead; end at Blue Point Roadhead.

Directions: From Dough Flat, follow closed Fire Road 6N16 easily uphill two miles to a "Y." Bear right and follow the dirt road to its end at a saddle where it becomes Trail 19W18. Follow this trail moderately downhill, switchbacking at times, to Ant Camp in 3.6 miles.

From oak-shaded Ant Camp, turn right (southeast) onto what remains of the Agua Blanca Trail (19W10), and hike mostly in the streambed for 1 mile to the site of Tin Can Cabin, where an early homesteader once constructed a makeshift cabin of battered five-gallon oil cans. Your route then climbs steeply and with difficulty around the Big Narrows, descends back into the canyon and reaches Cove Camp in 5 miles. It is possible but difficult to remain in the creek through the Narrows.

Continuing downstream, you pass the site of Hollister Camp in 2.8 miles and reach Log Cabin Camp in another mile. Climb above, or wade through, the Devil's Gateway, and hike along the creek to its confluence with the Piru, 3 miles away. There you bear south (right) and follow Piru Creek downstream 1 mile to the roadhead at Blue Point Campground.

TOPOS: *Devils Heart Peak, Cobblestone Mountain.* F/C

#35
A BACKPACK TO A HOT SPRING, AN INDIAN CAVE, AND A RUINED CABIN
25.3 Mile Loop

Description: Because maintenance funds are wanting, most long loop trips in the eastern portion of the Los Padres National Forest use unmaintained trails for at least part of their journey. The routes are often badly brushed over but can be readily followed using common sense and good routefinding techniques. This trip is no exception, and only experienced backpackers should undertake this strenuous hike. The rewards, however, are ample. You'll visit Sespe Hot Springs, the hottest natural spring in Southern California. You'll also explore the wild and seldom visited middle reaches of Sespe Creek along the edge of the Condor Sanctuary. There will be a Chumash Indian campsite with mysterious pictographs to experience, and also the ruins of an old miner's campsite at McDonald Cabin.

Make this a leisurely paced four-day trip with overnight stops at Sespe Hot Springs, Indian Cave, and Little Mutau camps.

Driving: Mutau Flat Roadhead.

Directions: From Mutau Flat, follow Trail 20W10 a short distance southeast to its junction with the Johnson Ridge Trail (20W12) and bear right. You follow this motorcycle trail on a moderate, bobbing descent down Johnson Ridge for five miles to the Old Sespe Road. The hot springs, where you can soak in the warm water, are 0.3 miles up the road to the left. The Hot Springs Camp is 0.3 miles down the road to the right. Rather than stay in the run-down camp, I prefer to bivouac on the sandy bench of Sespe Creek myself, which is only a short distance down canyon.

The second day of this outing begins with a short (0.4 miles) walk down the road from the camp. The road here makes a sharp bend to the right when it reaches Sespe Creek and heads upstream, but you should bear left at this point onto an old roadbed and follow it 0.4 miles to an unsigned junction. Bear left here onto the Alder Creek Trail (20W13), which climbs moderately over a ridge into the Alder

Creek drainage. There is a junction when the trail reaches the creek. The right fork goes a short distance to tiny Shady Camp, but you should stay to the left and travel upstream to Alder Creek Camp, a total of 5.1 miles so far for this hiking day. From there, continue 0.6 miles on the Alder Creek Trail (20W11) to a junction. Bear left and follow the pathway another 1.5 miles to Indian Cave Camp, where you can spend this night. Indian Cave is a mildly spooky campsite. To me it seems almost as if the "vibrations" of Chumash Indian spirits give the place a strange aura all its own.

Day three of your trek opens by resuming your upstream walk toward the headwaters of reliable Alder Creek. The trail is over-grown, brushy, even washed out in spots, but the route is always obvious. A mile-and-a-half beyond Indian Cave, the trail briefly detours up Sycamore Canyon and climbs quickly over a low hillock to bypass the narrows in the creek. It then descends back down into Alder Canyon, crosses the stream, and continues moderately uphill the remainder of the distance to McDonald Camp. Nearby are the ruins of a cabin dating back to the turn of the century. This distance between McDonald Camp and Indian Cave is 3.3 slow miles.

The going now gets tougher. From McDonald your route begins a steep switchbacking 2.1-mile ascent through chaparral toward the west. You pass the trickle from a seasonal spring and continue your climb out of the Alder Creek drainage to top a saddle at 6,100 feet. Just over this saddle is a trail junction. The connector trail to the right heads north to Alamo Mountain, but your route bears left and travels easily downhill along the Mutau Creek Trail (20W10) to your overnight destination at Little Mutau Camp 1.8 miles away along an intermittent stream.

Your final day on the trail is short, even if it involves some climbing. Just beyond Little Mutau, ascend west steeply to surmount a saddle in 1.8 miles. Proceed moderately to steeply downhill another two miles to Mutau Flat and your car.

TOPOS: *Lockwood Valley, Topatopa Mountain, Devils Heart Peak, McDonald Peak*

#36
EXPLORING THE MIDDLE SESPE COUNTRY
27 Miles One Way

Description: There are still some portions of Southern California that
are "de facto" wilderness areas, places that are wild and unspoiled
but do not yet have the protection of the Wilderness Act. One such
place is the mountain country north of Fillmore in Ventura County,
an area so wild it is the last refuge for the few remaining California
condors. While entry into the Sespe Refuge itself is not permitted,
travel through the Middle Sespe Creek country is allowed and will
be the focus of this trip. From the Condor Observation Point at Dough
Flat, you'll hike down to a camp in a secluded little canyon. You'll
then pay a visit to famous Sespe Hot Springs and hike upstream along
the Sespe across land once homesteaded by ranchers early in this
century.

Driving: Start at Dough Flat Roadhead; end at Lion Campground.

Directions: From the locked gate, walk up the Dough Flat Road (6N16)
for three miles, staying left at the "Y" to Cow Spring Camp. Hike
down into Alder Creek along Connector Trail 20W11 to a junction
below Dripping Springs, reached in 2.6 additional miles. Bear left onto
the Alder Creek Trail (20W13) to reach your first overnight stopover
at Alder Creek Camp. After settling in, a worthwhile side trip is
upstream 1.5 miles to the mysterious site of Indian Cave.
   On your next day, hike downstream along the creek an easy 0.7
miles and climb up over the canyon through the brushy chaparral. After
mounting a saddle, the trail descends moderately to an unmarked junction with an abandoned old road in 5.1 miles on the shore of Sespe
Creek. Follow the old roadbed and bear right into Hot Springs Canyon.
In 0.3 mile you pass a rundown trail camp and an additional 0.3 miles
farther on come to the hot spring itself. Extremely hot water, as hot
as 210 degrees Fahrenheit, boils out of a faulted fissure here. Although
temperatures are themselves intolerable, previous visitors have constructed a series of cooler downstream pools that are comfortable. The
nearby campground is a bit beat out for my taste. I prefer bivouacing

down along Sespe Creek itself. This also gets me away from the noise of the weekend bikers who ride in here along the Johnson Ridge Trail.

The rest of your hiking route is out along the remains of the Old Sespe Road (6N13), which follows the creek gently uphill for 15 miles to Lion Campground. This was once a four-wheel drive route to the springs, but it was made unusable to all but foot and pack traffic by floods in the late 1970s. All the old camps that were once along here have been removed.

Walk easily up the wide road and bivouac wherever you chose. There are many deep swimming holes at bends of the creek and numerous sandy flats on which to camp. I'd suggest allowing two days for this long trek in the shadow of the Topatopa Mountains to Lion Campground. But, under a forced march, a sturdy hiker could make it in a day.

TOPOS: *Devils Heart Peak, Lion Canyon, Topatopa Mountains*

#37
CEDARS, SPRUCE, AND FISHBOWLS
ALONG THE PIRU
13.1-Mile Loop

Description: This moderately easy, if long, overnight backpack will take you into the headwaters region of Piru Creek, where you will pass through three life zones—stream woodland, montane forest, chaparral—and probably encounter few hikers. Just a word of caution: During and after heavy rainfall, Piru Creek can swell to a torrent and the access road becomes a muddy mess. It is wise to avoid or leave the area if such a situation arises.

Driving: Thorn Meadows Roadhead.

Directions: Walk up closed Fireroad 22W10 on an easy, almost imperceptible ascent through the wide canyon of Piru Creek. At 2.5 miles the road turns to trail and you bear left to travel 0.6 miles to little Cedar Creek Camp on the Piru's south fork. Here at Cedar Creek, bigcone spruce, incense cedar, and a few live oaks provide the shade you're no doubt seeking; the quiet canyon, the seclusion. It makes a fine early lunch stop.

From the camp continue upstream on the same trail, climb moderately 1.2 miles to the top of a ridge where there is a trail junction. Bear right onto the Fishbowls Trail (22W05) and follow the conifer-forested ridge, climbing and dropping several times on a northwesterly heading. There are revealing open vistas along the way of the high forested country of the Mt. Piños District of the National Forest. After about a mile on this rollercoaster trail, you finally descend easily through a beautiful forest of spruce, cedar, juniper, and pine to Fishbowls Camp on Piru Creek, 2.5 miles from Cedar Creek. The best spot to lay out your gear is on the wide flat across the creek from the signed camp.

Eons ago, when this land was under the sea, sand and other silts were deposited as sediment. The pressure of hundreds of feet of sea water eventually formed this sediment into the rocks you see today. Ironically, rock formed in this fashion is soft and easily eroded by moving water and evidence of this process is what you will find at the Fishbowls. The backcountry site gets its name from a series of small but deep pools worn into the sandstone by Piru Creek over the centuries. These pools, just upstream from the camp, are deep enough for a quick dip, should the day prove warm enough. Since they are deep as well as narrow, they represent an excellent opportunity to study stream ecology. On my first trip into this area many years ago, I met a half dozen USC biology students who had come to this place for that very purpose.

After a restful night under the conifers of the Fishbowls, you should plan for a lazy, hardy breakfast since the way back is easy and downhill. Continue downstream from camp on a trail that soon turns into a jeep road. Strolling along the 6.2 miles to the Grade Valley Road, you might just run across a weekend goldminer or two, sluicing or panning in the sandy shallows. In the boom years at the turn of the century, this valley was the scene of extensive placer mining activities as hundreds of men sought their fortune. As gold has risen in price, more than a few individuals still try their luck during good weather.

When you reach the Grade Valley Road, walk or hitchhike your way 0.5 miles south to the Thorn Meadows spur road and then west 0.7 miles back to your car.

TOPOS: *San Guillermo, Lockwood Valley*

#38
FROM THE SESPE TO THE PIRU
13 Miles One Way

Description: Stretching from the watershed of Sespe Creek into the headwaters of the Piru, this trip travels through chaparral, canyon woodland, and pine forest. On weekdays the area is generally peaceful and deserted, and I highly recommend it for a two-day outing with an overnight campout at Pine Mountain Lodge. A long car shuttle is necessary, however.

Driving: Start at Lion Roadhead; end at Thorn Meadows.

Directions: From Lion Campground, cross Sespe Creek and follow the Piedra Blanca Trail (22W03) through chaparral for 1 mile. You then descend to Piedra Blanca Creek and hike through stream woodland for another 1.4 miles to Twin Forks Camp. After a steep 2.9-mile ascent of the north fork of the Piedra Blanca, you reach homey Pine Mountain Lodge Camp where you'll spend the night. The stars and the view are outstanding at this high elevation.

After your night on Pine Mountain, turn northeast at a junction just above camp onto the Cedar Creek Trail (22W10) and hike over a ridge to a junction. Bear right here and follow this pleasant footpath (21W06) 3.8 miles downhill into Cedar Creek Camp. From there, continue 0.6 miles downstream, bearing right onto a fire road, and hike the remaining 2.5 miles to Thorn Meadows Roadhead, your shuttle point.

Except for the long climb up to the Lodge Camp, this should be considered a fairly easy trip.

TOPOS: *Lion Canyon, San Guillermo, Lockwood Valley*

#39
AN EASY HIKE DOWN FROM MT. PIÑOS
9.6 Miles One Way

Description: This shuttle trip down from the summit of Mt. Piños to Three Falls Boy Scout Camp is an enjoyable if long downhill day hike, an easy overnight backpack trip with the choice of two trail camps, and an excellent conditioning hike to get you acclimated and in shape for adventures in the Sierra Nevada and elsewhere. Snow blankets the higher sections of this route from late December through March.

Driving: Start at Mt. Piños; end at Three Falls BSA Camp.

Directions: From the top of Mt. Piños, follow Trail 21W03 down a draw and up Sawmill Mountain. you reach a junction in 2 miles, where you bear left onto the North Fork Trail (22W02) and travel down to Sheep Camp in an easy 0.5 miles. The well-maintained trail continues another 3 miles downhill to Lilly Meadows Camp. It's then only another 4.1 miles, via trail and fireroad, to your car at Three Falls BSA Camp.

TOPO: *Sawmill Mountain*

#40
PINE MOUNTAIN TO THORN MEADOWS
16.1 Miles One Way

Description: This moderate trek, suitable for anyone in good condition, travels along the ridge of Pine Mountain where you can enjoy wide-ranging vistas of the canyon of Sespe Creek and the Cuyama Valley. From Reyes Peak, you'll hike downhill to the headwaters of Piedra Blanca Creek. You'll then traverse a low divide and drop to Cedar Creek, at the headwaters of the Piru. Snow closes the area in winter. I suggest allowing two full days for this shuttle trip, with an overnight stopover at Pine Mountain Lodge.

Driving: Start at Reyes Peak Roadhead; end at Thorn Meadows.

Directions: From the end of the Pine Mountain Road, hike briefly along a closed fire road to the Reyes Peak Trail (23W04), which takes off to the left. Follow this ridgetop route through chaparral and a forest of white fir and pondrosa pine descending easily to Haddock Camp 3.5 miles from the start. At the trail junction in camp bear right onto the Piedra Blanca Trail (22W03) and continue for 3.4 miles past Three Mile Camp to the attractive campsite at Pine Mountain Lodge. Spend your night here.

From the junction above camp, turn left (northeast) onto the Cedar Creek Trail (22W10) and climb over a saddle into the drainage of Piru Creek. At another junction bear right and descend easily to reach shady Cedar Creek Camp in 3.8 miles. From the camp follow the trail downstream for 0.6 miles and then bear right down the closed fire road 2.5 miles to Thorn Meadows Roadhead, your shuttle point.

TOPOS: *Reyes Peak, San Guillermo, Lockwood Valley, Lion Canyon*

#41
FROM PINE MOUNTAIN DOWN TO THE SESPE
14.5 Miles One Way

Description: This shuttle trip provides a fine overview of the drainage of Sespe Creek. It's also a backpacker's dream: Almost every step of the trek is downhill. From Reyes Peak on Pine Mountain you'll travel along a forested ridgetop and then descend to the pleasant canyon of Piedra Blanca Creek. After a good night's rest at Three Mile Camp, you'll then descend the cool canyon of the Piedra Blanca to Lion Campground on the Sespe. Allow two days for this hike.

Since this is by almost any standard an easy hike, take your time and use it to let the wild backcountry work on you. Pause along Pine Mountain Ridge to watch the sun glisten through the clusters of ponderosa pine needles as the wind caresses their bows. Enjoy the star-studded night as you repose at the high elevation of Three Mile Camp. Sit back at Twin Falls and experience the music of the falling water. Relax.

Driving: Start at Reyes Peak Roadhead; end at Lion Campground.

Directions: From the locked gate on the Pine Mountain Road hike briefly along the fire road and bear left onto the ridgetop Reyes Peak Trail (23W04), which you follow a moderate 5.8 miles down to Haddock Camp on Piedra Blanca Creek. Bear right at the junction here onto the Piedra Blanca Trail (22W03) and hike 1.6 miles to your overnight destination at little Three Mile Camp, an attractive site shaded by ponderosa pine and incense cedar.

In the morning, continue down the Piedra Blanca Trail 1.8 miles to Pine Mountain Lodge and, bearing right at the junction, top a small rise and descend moderately 2.9 miles along the creek's north fork to Twin Forks Camp. You then follow the creek downhill 1.4 miles past Piedra Blanca Camp, climb briefly around some handsome sandstone buttresses, and descend 1 mile to Lion Campground on Sespe Creek.

TOPOS: *Lion Canyon, Reyes Peak, San Guillermo*

#42
DOWN THE CHORRO GRANDE
5.3 Miles One Way

Description: Should you be taking a companion out for his or her first overnight excursion and want an easy yet scenic area to visit, by all means consider shallow Chorro Grande Canyon. Distances are short, roads are close by, and water available. This downhill hike also passes through three life zones—conifer forest, chaparral, and stream woodland—providing an opportunity to observe a variety of contrasts. The hike is best in spring when wildflowers lend their color to the slopes. Summers are hot. There is snow here in winter. You could easily do this trip as a dayhike; however, if backpacking, I suggest an overnight stop at little Oak Camp.

Driving: Start at Reyes Peak Roadhead; end at Chorro Grande.

Directions: From Reyes Peak Campground at the roadhead, follow the Chorro Grande Trail (23W05) moderately downhill through ponderosa pine and white fir for 1 mile to Chorro Grande Camp where an icy spring gushes out from beneath a large boulder. As you walk down the switchbacking trail beyond camp, there is a wide vista to enjoy of the valley of Sespe Creek and Highway 33 far below. You soon enter the chaparral belt, where scattered bigcone spruce make their appearance in 1.5 miles, and then a dirt road. If you explore upstream to the right here, you will find the small flat that used to shelter Three Pines Camp before it was washed out on schedule in the heavy 1973 rains. But your route travels left downhill (on the dirt road) and continues on a straight bearing through a confusing junction of dirt roads that have scarred the mountainside. The footpath picks up shortly on the right and takes you to shady Oak Camp in a quick and easy 0.4 miles of descent. A seasonal creek flows through here, fed by the spring of Chorro Grande. Why not spend the night?

The easy descent from Oak Camp passes through a forest of streamside alders. The route then widens into a jeep road that continues down toward the Felt Ranch. Watch to the right, however, and follow the obvious trail that appears after a short distance. Hike on it through chaparral and a number of stream crossings to reach Chorro Grande Roadhead, your shuttle point, in 2 miles.

TOPOS: *Wheeler Springs, Reyes Peak*

The turkey vulture, close cousin to the condor, is often mistaken for one of the rare big birds. (U.S. FOREST SERVICE)

#43
CREEK-HOPPING NORTH OF PINE MOUNTAIN
18.4 Miles One Way

Description: This backpack trip explores the drainages on the northern slopes of Pine Mountain. It passes through the watersheds of Reyes, Beartrap, Piedra Blanca, Cedar, and Piru creeks. In spring the streams are all at full flow and a few snow patches may even be encountered among the wildflowers. This is a moderately strenuous hike with a lot of elevation gain and loss. A group in good shape could hike the route in two days, staying overnight at Haddock Camp. But if you'd prefer to take it more slowly, there are plenty of trail camps along the way.

Driving: Start at Reyes Creek Roadhead; end at Thorn Meadows.

Directions: From the Reyes Creek Campground, follow the Beartrap Trail (23W02) up over a ridge, then down to Upper Reyes Camp in 3.5 miles. The route then travels upstream and switchbacks over a second ridge to descend into Beartrap Canyon and Beartrap Camp at 1.5 miles. After continuing up the cool canyon an easy mile, you then ascend to a third saddle and drop down to Haddock on Piedra Blanca Creek in 2.1 miles. This is your halfway point.

Hiking onto the Piedra Blanca Trail (22W03), walk downstream past Three Mile Camp and onto beautiful Pine Mountain Lodge in 3.4 miles. Just above the Lodge Camp, bear left onto the Cedar Creek Trail (22W10) and hike over a ridge to a junction with the Fishbowls Trail. Bear right here and descend to shady Cedar Creek Camp, a good lunch stop, in 3.8 miles. From this point, travel downstream for 0.6 miles and bear right onto a fire road that takes you in 2.5 miles to the Thorn Meadows Roadhead, your shuttle point.

TOPOS: *Reyes Peak, San Guillermo, Lockwood Valley, Lion Canyon*

#44
FROM REYES PEAK TO REYES CREEK
13.9 Miles One Way

Description: Descending the northern slopes of Pine Mountain through the drainages of three of its creeks, this shuttle trip is cool and pleasant in early spring. You'll enjoy pine forest, chaparral, and stream woodland during this moderate hike, which is mostly downhill. You should allow two days for this trek, with your overnight stop at Beartrap Camp.

Driving: Start at Reyes Peak Roadhead; end at Reyes Creek.

Directions: From the locked gate at the end of the Pine Mountain Road at Reyes Peak, walk a short distance on the closed fire road and bear left on the Reyes Peak Trail (23W04). Follow this ridgetop route 5.8 easy miles down to Haddock Camp. At the junction in camp, bear left (northwest), climb over a saddle, and descend into the drainage of Beartrap Creek on the Beartrap Trail (23W02). You pass the site of long gone Beartrap No. 2 Camp in 2 miles and continue down the cool canyon another mile to Beartrap No. 1, your overnight stop.

The following morning, continue downstream briefly, then climb moderately 300 feet up and over a ridge to descend via switchbacks into Upper Reyes Camp in 1.5 miles. Cross the creek and climb one mile to a saddle. Then, enjoying the views out to the arid Cuyama Badlands, a product of heavy erosion near the San Andreas Fault, descend the final 2.5 miles to your shuttle point at Reyes Creek Campground.

TOPOS: *Reyes Peak, San Guillermo*

#45
A GREAT MEAL AND AN
EARLY SEASON WORKOUT
7.9 Miles One Way

Description: There are those who like to stretch their legs and get ready for the Sierra with an early season backpack into the local mountains. And there are those who, while on the trail, savor the most elaborate gourmet fare. And there are those who like to combine both, but dread the inevitable backbreaking drudge of carrying a ten-pound turkey with all the trimmings eight miles to some remote camp. On this trek I'll show you how to have it both ways—a good meal and a good workout. From Highway 33 you'll head up a fairly easy trail to a camp only a couple miles off the road on the slopes of the Sierra Madre. Then, fortified by a hearty dinner, you'll return to civilization the following morning by a different route through a corner of the Dick Smith Wilderness. So start planning that menu and packing that pack. One note of caution: This will be a dry camp, so be sure to bring along plenty of drinking water.

Driving: Start at Ozena Roadhead; end at Rancho Nueva.

Directions: From Ozena Roadhead hike up the wide and well-marked Deal Canyon Trail (24W04), really a retiring dirt road, named for a prospector who sought out uranium in this area during the post-war years. You climb first easily then a bit more moderately up Bear Canyon, gradually leaving the sound of traffic on Highway 33 far behind. Two miles from the roadhead, you walk into Mine Camp. Here, in the shade of bigcone spruce and a smattering of piñon pine, unshoulder your pack and set to work preparing your feast. It's highly unlikely you'll have any unexpected dinner guests. Except during hunting season, this corner of the Los Padres rarely sees visitors.

In the morning, your weighty provisions consumed and ready to fuel another day, cinch up your greatly lightened backpack and continue hiking uphill a short distance. At 4,650 feet, you cross over a shallow divide and enter the drainage of Deal Canyon. Your trek is all downhill from here.

Backpackers pause for a rest along the Santa Cruz Trail in the San Rafael Wilderness. (U.S. FOREST SERVICE)

As you descend along the easy trail, enjoy this pleasant walk back to the Cuyama Valley. In springtime colorful stands of wildflowers—lupine, paintbrush, poppy—favor this cool north-facing canyon. Bigcone and piñon stand like sentinels on the high mountain ridges. Four and a half miles beyond Mine Camp, you reach Deal Junction Camp on Rancho Nuevo Creek. Turn right here and hike down the Rancho Nuevo Trail (24W03) a quick and easy 1.4 miles to your second car. **TOPOS:** *Rancho Nuevo Creek, Reyes Peak.* W/A

#46
A TREK DOWN MATILIJA CANYON
7.1 Miles One Way

Description: Equally refreshing as a day hike or as a lazy weekend backpack, this route tours the heavily chaparral-covered slopes of Ortega Hill. As the trail winds down the storm-scarred north fork of Matilija Creek, the eroded canyon walls clearly reveal the workings of the Santa Ynez Fault in the tilt of the sedimentary layers. Bigcone spruce and western chokecherry appear in spots on the northern slopes of Ortega. There are a few fire-blackened pines near the summit, and live oaks are abundant through most of the canyon. Although badly burned during the Wheeler Fire of 1985, the area is recovering nicely. There will be some washouts in the trail where the winter rains did their damage. You may elect to spend the night either at Maple or Middle Matilija Camps.

Driving: Start at Cherry Creek Roadhead; end at Matilija.

Directions: From the end of the Cherry Creek Road, follow the fire road past a locked gate. Continue onto the Matilija Trail (23W07) for a brief climb up to a saddle at 4,979 feet. There is a junction here with the Ortega Motorcycle Trail to the left. From here also, the remaining 650 feet to the summit of Ortega Hill can be climbed most easily from the south. Those who take the time will find the views in all directions quite rewarding.

The Matilija Trail continues downhill from the saddle, descending to Maple Camp, 0.6 miles from the roadhead, where shade is provided by bigleaf maple trees. You continue on a sometimes steep descent down the narrow-walled canyon, passing the abandoned site of Upper Matilija Camp and reaching Middle Matilija on a sizeable streamside flat in 3 miles. Shortly after the camp, the trail becomes an old jeep road (badly washed out) and travels above the streambed to the popular picnic site of Matilija Camp, 2.5 miles distant. Stratification of the canyon walls is especially evident here. From this final camp, follow the road out into Matilija Canyon and, bearing left, travel, via streambed and road, downstream to Matilija Roadhead, 1 mile away.

TOPOS: *Wheeler Spring, Old Man Mountain.* F/C

#47
THE OCEAN VIEW LOOP
16.5-Mile Loop

Description: There is a certain joy that comes from being in high places, a feeling of freedom that must be akin to what birds experience in flight. A trek along the Ocean View Trail atop the Santa Ynez Mountains is one of those places to which a hiker can come to share in that experience.

From the 2,000-foot level at Juncal Campground, you will climb over 2,700 feet in 7.5 miles to Divide Peak to enjoy that feeling of being on top of the world. As you hike along the crest of the Santa Ynez Mountains, you will see far off ocean ripples turn into foaming waves crashing on what appears to be a miniature shoreline almost a mile below. You will watch miniature cars crawl slowly along the ribbon of Pacific Coast Highway. You will view soft white cumulus clouds billowing over the high peaks of the distant San Rafael and Dick Smith wildernesses. If you are very fortunate you may witness a magnificent condor soaring in flight on the westerly winds. And all around you, the dark green carpet of heavy chaparral will serve to insulate you from the cares and woes of the harried, now seemingly remote, day-to-day world. Unfortunately, a portion of the Ocean View Trail is a designated motorcycle route within the National Forest. On weekends the machines may give your sense of peace a bit of competition. I suggest you do this trip as a two-day backpack with an overnight stop at Upper Santa Ynez Camp.

Driving: Juncal Roadhead.

Directions: From Juncal Campground follow the Santa Ynez Fire Road (5N13) east past the locked gate and continue on an easy climb 6.3 miles past Juncal Dam, Jameson Lake, Billiard Flats and on to Upper Santa Ynez Camp. Little is left of the old campsite, but you will find a stove and reliable water here. The road on which you have traveled was one of those built in the 1930s by the C.C.C. as a way of opening up the backcountry and was part of the main overland route to Ojai.

The following morning, continue up the fire road to the Murietta Divide. There turn south onto the Monte Arido Trail and climb steeply 0.8 miles through chaparral charred in the 1985 Wheeler Fire up to a ridgetop firebreak known as the Ocean View Trail (24W08). Turn right here and continue on this crest fire break along the ridge of the Santa Ynez Mountains on a tiring up and down hike. All the while you will be enjoying aerial views of Santa Barbara, Carpinteria, Ventura, and Oxnard, as well as far out to the Channel Islands. To the north, you will witness the rugged peaks and canyons of the wilderness backcountry. Be sure to take a map along, because you may want to identify the interesting places your eyes pick out. A map will also be helpful in locating the upper end of the Franklin Trail, which will be your route of return.

As the Ocean View Trail winds to the west, it passes just below the summits of Divide (4,707 feet) and Noon (4,084 feet) peaks. Both are easily climbed. After 5 miles of rollercoaster hiking, just as you pass directly above blue Jameson Lake and sight some power lines ahead, turn right onto the unsigned Franklin Trail (25W09). Follow it north down a ridgeline into the drainage of small Alder Creek. At the 3,000-foot level, the Franklin Trail joins Alder Creek and follows the stream back down past a camp to the Santa Ynez Fire Road, 2 miles from the crest. Turn left onto this road and retrace your steps 2.4 miles back to Juncal Campground.

TOPOS: *White Ledge Peak, Carpinteria.* F/C

#48
THROUGH BLUE CANYON TO COLD SPRING SADDLE
7.4 Miles One Way

Description: If asked to suggest an easy backpack trip in the mountains near Santa Barbara during the springtime, my first choice would be little Blue Canyon. Just over the crest of the Santa Ynez Mountains from town, this is an easy and pleasant overnighter, suitable for just about anyone. Why not take a weekend and spend your days at any of the four trail camps along this route?

Driving: Start at Blue Canyon Roadhead; end at Cold Spring.

Directions: Follow the Blue Canyon Trail (26W12) west easily above the creek for 0.9 miles to Upper Blue Canyon Camp. Your route then continues downstream, on a partially washed out but easily followed route, to rustic and shady Blue Canyon Camp, 1.5 miles farther. Another 1.7 miles along this same trail will take you into Cottam Camp. Bear left here onto the Forbush Canyon Trail (26W13) and begin a moderate climb west upcanyon 1.6 miles to Forbush Camp, an old homesteader's site. Here in camp you connect with the Cold Spring Trail (27W10) and follow it south moderately uphill for 1.7 miles to East Camino Cielo at Cold Spring Saddle, your shuttle point.
TOPOS: *Santa Barbara, Carpinteria*

#49
IN THE FOOTSTEPS OF THE CHUMASH
23.1 Miles One Way

Description: When the Spanish established the mission system in Alta California in the late 1700s, they used it primarily to control the native Indian population. It was felt that the civilizing influence of Christianity and the stability of an organized work force would minimize conflicts between the natives and settlers. And to some extent the program worked. Robberies and raids declined and the settlements prospered. Yet the Indians harbored a certain resentment against the soldiers whom they regarded as their captors. Despite the molifying influence of the padres, this friction was destined to some day explode. Writes historian Jim Blakley: "With the dawning of the year 1824 conditions for an Indian revolt were ripening. The missionaries treated the Indians as children in their care, but the soldiers used and harassed the Indians at every opportunity. They requisitioned the Indians for work details with little or no recompense. The slightest infraction of rules brought on swift and severe punishment."

The keg exploded on February 21, 1824. Amid reports that an Indian had been whipped by a guard, a general revolt began at Mission Santa Ynez. Property and lives were lost. Although initially crushed by the militia, the revolt spread the following day to Mission Santa Barbara. Laden with provisions, the Indians fled up Mission Canyon to the Santa Ynez River and headed upstream. Following an ancient trail up Mono Canyon, they reached freedom in the San Joaquin Valley near the site of present-day Buena Vista Lake.

To quell fears of any additional revolt among the valley tribes, Lt. Narciso Fabregat was dispatched with a force to recapture the errant tribe. He failed dismally. A second expedition was then dispatched under the command of Capt. Pablo de la Portillo, who met with more success. By early June, Portillo had located the rebels. He was not only backed by a strong military force but had the good sense to bring along two mission padres. Together they convinced the Chumash to return to Santa Barbara.

The group headed back to the coast on June 16 and reached the mission six days later. On their way they followed the ancient Chumash trail. On this hike you'll walk in their footsteps as you backpack along the Mono-Alamar Trail through the Dick Smith Wilderness.

Driving: Start at Mono Roadhead; end at Santa Barbara Canyon.

Directions: From the locked gate at Little Caliente Hot Springs, the Mono-Alamar Trail follows Fire Road 5N33 and then Jeep Road 6N30 north on an easy grade. In 3.6 miles you pass the private Ogilvy Ranch, which in mission times was the location of the Chumash Village of Siquawa, also called San Gervasio by the Spanish. Beyond here, the road gradually reverts to a trail (27W07) and travels through several crossings of Mono Creek to reach Mono Narrows Trail Camp 6.8 miles from the start. Plan to spend your first night here. If daylight and ambition permit, spend some time exploring the pools and falls upstream in the narrow canyon.

The next morning continue north on the Mono-Alamar Trail (26W08) climbing up a tributary stream. In less than a mile you begin to ascend out of the canyon over a steep rock formation known since Spanish times as the Caracole (''spiral staircase''). Two and one-half miles beyond the Narrows you come to a junction. To the left here is the route into upper Indian Canyon; you bear right, however, to cross over Alamar Hill and descend through chaparral 1.5 miles to Lower Alamar Camp. So far you've come 4 miles this hiking day, and this camp makes a good lunch stop to refuel for the hard trek ahead.

As of this writing, the trail beyond here is in poor shape and badly brushed over. It is scheduled for maintenance in the fall of 1986. Hike north on the Mono-Alamar Trail (26W05 and 26W06) upcanyon through numerous stream crossings. In about a mile you bisect an old jeep road and in 3.2 miles reach Dutch Oven Camp on an oak-shaded flat along Mono Creek. This is your stopover point, and as you lay out your gear for the night you might reflect on this area's history. Because of its location midway between the coast and Central Valley, Dutch Oven was long used as a campsite by the Indians, Spanish, and Anglos alike. Near or perhaps even at this site was the Chumash village of Casitec, known to the Spanish as San Pablo. It is known that the Portillo party, returning from the San Joaquin Valley in 1824 camped here. It was a favorite hunting retreat for the Cord brothers of Ventura here. It was a favorite hunting retreat for the Cord brothers of Ventura County, and the place got its name from a broken dutch oven they once left here.

The following day, the distance is short on a recently improved trail. From Dutch Oven continue north on the increasingly steep trail (26W20). After 2 miles of climbing you top a ridge known as the Puerta Suela (Gateway) on a flank of Madulce Peak and then drop down into Pine Canyon. Bear left onto the Madulce Trail (25W03) and hike the easy path a short distance to Madulce Cabin and Camp. Enjoy the rest of your day as a layover in the cool shade of the ponderosa pines, bigcone spruce, and incense cedars. It's interesting to explore the historic cabin (see trip #50). The truly footloose might want to challenge Madulce Peak (6,536 feet) for some truly outstanding views. the Santa Barbara Cañyon Roadhead at Cox Flat.

TOPOS: *Hildreth Peak, Madulce Peak, Little Pine Mountain.* W/A

#50
A BACKPACK ON THE NORTHERN
SLOPES OF MADULCE PEAK
23-Mile Loop

Description: Pablo de la Portillo was probably the first white man to visit the vicinity of Big Pine Mountain when he passed through this corner of the Santa Barbara Backcountry in search of the runaway renegade Chumash in 1824. But the Mono-Alamar Trail through this area had been used for centuries by the Indians as their main north-south route for trading with inland tribes.

With the passage of the Homestead Act, squatters began wandering through here after the Civil War. One of them, named Old Marlowe, was the first to settle at the place we know today as Madulce Flats. He built a cabin in the 1880s and lived there for several years only to move on and disappear in 1890. After the proclamation of the Forest Preserve in 1898, the cabin was converted into a guard station and used as a house and office for patroling rangers. The old structure was finally torn down in 1929 and replaced by a more sturdy building of shiplap and clapboard hauled in by mules. Although abandoned in 1941, it was repaired by the Forest Service in 1980 and is now listed on the National Register of Historic Places.

On your first night of this three-day loop, you will visit the Madulce Cabin deep in the Dick Smith Wilderness. You'll then climb over Madulce Ridge and follow the Sisquoc River from its headwaters down to Heath Camp in the San Rafael Wilderness. Your final day will be spent climbing up to the top of the Sierra Madres, where you'll follow a fire road back to the start.

Driving: Santa Barbara Canyon Roadhead.

Directions: Follow the Mono-Alamar Trail (25W02), an old jeep road, south up Santa Barbara Canyon. The going is generally moderate with numerous stream crossings. At 4.5 miles from the start, the trail heads up a tributary canyon and, climbing more steeply, tops a ridge before descending easily into the beautiful little valley along Pine Creek where you'll find both the famous Madulce Cabin and a nearby campground.

Stream water is generally reliable, but there is a spring aways behind the cabin just in case. Shade is provided by bigcone spruce, ponderosa pine, and incense cedar.

Day two begins with a trek up Pine Canyon on the Madulce Trail (25W03), which climbs through a conifer forest to meet the Big Pine Road (9N11) in 2.5 miles. Turn south here and hike an easy mile to Alamar Saddle. Turn west and descend onto the Sisquoc Trail (27W07) and plan to enjoy a thoroughly pleasant day of hiking. After entering the San Rafael Wilderness, the trail first passes the turnoff to Bear Camp where the Sisquoc's headwaters bubble out of the ground. A short distance on is Lower Bear, set at the edge of a large tree-lined meadow. Just beyond is the notorious Devil's Slide, an area of unstable shale that caused nothing but trouble for the early pioneers. Before this trail, the slide was so steep one didn't dare try to ride a horse up it. In the opposite direction, riders dismounted and skidded their horses down. Your route switchbacks steeply down the trail to the foot of the cliff where you may pause to enjoy streamside Upper Sisquoc Falls Camp along with its spectacular waterfall. From here it's 3 easy miles and 10 stream crossings downriver to Heath Camp, your stop for the night. This site is shaded by oaks and sycamores and was a favored retreat of old Jim Heath, a local rancher and friend of Teddy Roosevelt.

Your final day is long and largely uphill, so get an early start. From Heath Camp, head up the brushy Judell Trail (25W05). It wastes no time climbing through the chaparral along the route of an intermittent stream, gaining Santa Barbara Potrero in 4.7 miles. Turn right onto the Sierra Madre Road (32S13) and follow it a short ways to the Big Pine Road (9N11). Turn left and walk the remaining 3 miles back to your car.

TOPOS: *Madulce Peak, Big Pine Mountain, Fox Mountain, Salisbury Potrero.* F/C, W/A

#51
THE SOUTHERN LOOP THROUGH THE
SAN RAFAEL WILDERNESS
64.6-Mile Loop

Description: If you have a week off from work or school next spring, don't waste it partying in Palm Springs or scorching your skin on the beach. Instead come to the land of booming creeks, deep swimming holes, high mountain pine forests, and crystal clear air. Come experience the backcountry in this southern corner of the San Rafael Wilderness. On this trip you will travel through 35 square miles of this primitive area in a seven-day backpack. Elevations ranging from 1,225 feet at the roadhead to nearly 6,500 feet atop West Big Pine Mountain will expose you to all of the life zones and climatic experiences the Santa Barbara Backcountry has to offer. Allow at least seven or perhaps even ten days for this trip with overnight stopovers at Happy Hollow, Flores, Mission Pine Spring, Bear, Pelch, and Santa Cruz camps. You should be in good condition.

Driving: Upper Oso Roadhead.

Directions: From the campground follow the Camuesa Fire Road (5N15) 0.8 miles uphill. Turn left on the Santa Cruz Trail (27W09) and hike on up Oso Canyon along the gurgling stream. After passing the short spur trail to Nineteen Oaks Camp, the Santa Cruz Trail begins a steep switchbacking ascent in and out of shallow canyons and continues to Alexander Saddle 5 miles from the start. You then follow an old bulldozer road up to Happy Hollow Camp, your first night's stopover. There is no water here.

The second hiking day begins with a brisk 5.5-mile descent by way of ridgetop, chaparral slope, and canyon to beautiful Santa Cruz Camp, the southern gateway into the San Rafael Wilderness. The pristine surroundings might tempt you to spend the day at Santa Cruz, but I suggest continuing on to an equally lovely spot for your second night. From the camp continue along the Santa Cruz Trail (27W09) northwest up Black Canyon, then veer off due north to complete a 1.2-mile ascent to the top of a ridge that marks the wilderness area boundary.

Stay right at the junction with the spur trail to Santa Cruz Peak, and descend an easy 1.6 miles to one of my favorite retreats, Flores Camp.

Flores is named for a homesteader who, around the turn of the century, happened upon this beautiful meadowed spot and decided to stake his claim. He built a ten-by-twelve-foot frame cabin with a shake roof and a dirt floor and lived here five years to qualify for his patent. He raised cattle and crops and lived a healthy life of a mountain man. The camp where you will spend the night is located along the creek at the site of the Flores Cabin.

Your third day on the trail will be one of heavy climbing and I suggest you start at dawn. Leaving Flores, hike along the Santa Cruz Trail (27W09) upstream to a trail junction. You bear right, cross over a low hill and join Coche Creek. The trail follows the creek upstream through a half dozen stream crossings 3 miles to Coche Camp. Rest here and fill your canteens brim full. There will be no more water until your evening campsite.

Take a deep breath and continue up the steep switchbacking Santa Cruz Trail for a hot and tiring 3.8 miles heading due north. At the end of the climb, which seems much longer than it actually is, you top a rise and descend briefly into Mission Pine Basin. With its tall inspiring ponderosa pine, bigcone spruce, and incense cedar forest, the basin is a perfect campsite except for one thing: no easily accessible water. (In a pinch, you can find water at a reliable spring in Fall Creek Canyon, about a mile to the north, at the site of an old hunter's camp called Cooper.)

I suggest, after resting sufficiently, you head west on the Mission Pine Trail (28W01) toward Mission Pine Spring. You will be climbing gently as you hike along the chaparral-covered crest enjoying fantastic views and a gentle cooling breeze the entire 3.3-mile distance to a campsite that does have everything. When you reach Mission Pine Spring, I think you will agree that the day's 10-mile hike was well worth the effort and, in fact, may choose to lay over a day in this beautiful subalpine setting at nearly 6,000 feet. If you do lay over, consider climbing 6,593-foot San Rafael Mountain nearby. You can do it easily by continuing west along the Mission Pine Trail an additional 2.2 miles.

Your fourth hiking day will be long, high, and largely dry. Fill your canteens. From Mission Pine Spring retrace your steps eastward, gently descending the 3.3 miles back to Mission Pine Basin. Then continue east on the Mission Pine Trail (28W01), staying on top of the ridge between San Rafael and Big Pine Mountains. You climb moderately for the first mile, then gently descend for another 2 miles. You then undertake a 1,000-foot climb to the top of 6,490-foot West Big Pine Peak. The climb starts out steep, then levels out a bit. From the peak you then descend 1.4 miles, partly along a retired roadbed, to the Big Pine Fire Road (9N11) where you can find reliable water at the spring at Big Pine Camp, a quarter-mile off the road.

Turn left and follow the Big Pine Road 2.2 miles as it contours around Big Pine Mountain and, heading north, descends to a junction with the upper Sisquoc River Trail (27W07). Turn left onto this trail and follow it downhill 1.5 miles to Lower Bear Camp, about one-half mile from the spring that is the headwaters of the Sisquoc River. Set on the edge of a grassy meadow and surrounded by tall healthy pines, Bear Camp may lead you into thinking you've stopped in the Sierra Nevada. Again, you may wish to lay over here for a day. If you do, be sure to explore Upper Sisquoc Falls just a short way downstream.

For your fifth hiking day on this wilderness trek, retrace your steps 1.5 miles back up to the Big Pine Fire Road, then travel south 2.8 miles back to the Mission Pine Trail. From there continue southwesterly along the Big Pine Road 3 miles to Bluff Camp where there is a junction with the Grapevine Trail (27W10). Turn right here and follow this trail downhill 3 miles to Pelch Camp set on a flat along Grapevine Creek. Pelch is the site of yet another hunting camp built by partners Pelch and Pinkham in the 1930s. Back in those days they used to pack in all their gear along with a healthy supply of Golden Glow Ale and pennies for pincohle. They'd hunt for camp meat here near their cabin and head up into Mission Pine Basin for the real trophy bucks. There is little left of their then elaborate camp, but I suggest you overnight here at this true wilderness site.

Your sixth hiking day is long but largely downhill and it covers much familiar territory. From Pelch, head northwest on the Grapevine Trail (27W10). You hike along the east fork upstream, then cross and ascend up and over a ridge. After descending via switchbacks, you hike along and then ford Grapevine Creek twice, passing Jackrabbit Flats, to reach Coche Camp near a trail junction, 3 miles from Pelch. For the rest of this trip you will be retracing your steps. Following the Santa Cruz

Trail (27W09), descend 3 miles to Flores Flats, then climb over the
ridge and continue to Santa Cruz Camp, 2.8 miles. Spend your final
night here.

For the last day of your weeklong trek, follow the Santa Cruz Trail
11.5 miles up and over Alexander Saddle near Little Pine Mountain,
then descend back down to Upper Oso Roadhead.

TOPOS: *Big Pine Mountain, San Rafael Mountain, San Marcos Pass,
Little Pine Mountain.* F/C, W/A

*The Santa Ynez River, with its innumerable fishing and swimming
pools, is a major gateway into the Santa Barbara Backcountry.*
(BLAKLEY ARCHIVES)

#52
A TWO-DAY TRIP TO WHITE LEDGE CAMP
25-Mile Loop

Description: This trek into the San Rafael Wilderness is a study in contrasts. From the lush, well-watered canyon of Manzana Creek you will follow an old Chumash Indian route up to White Ledge Camp, then return via the barren summit of Hurricane Deck and the dry canyon of Lost Valley. For a good part of the way, no water will be available at all. Hikes such as this were commonplace for the ancient Indians, who performed them without out the aid of backpacks, lug-soled boots, or sleeping bags. This trip makes a strenuous two-day outing with an overnight campout at White Ledge Camp. On the return leg, you may wish to explore the Indian site at Pool Rock or Condor Cave. See Trip #12 for directions to these sites.

Driving: NIRA Roadhead.

Directions: From the end of the campground, cross the creek and hike up the Manzana Trail (30W13) over a low ridge guarded by digger pines to Lost Valley Camp, 1 mile away. There is a junction on the left here with the Lost Valley Trail, which will be your route of return, but for this part of the hike continue up the Manzana Trail southeast along the creek. You pass a junction with a spur path leading to Fish Creek Camp in 2.4 miles, then descend to a crossing and continue along the opposite bank.

After additionally crossing several tributaries, you reach oak- and manzanita-shaded Manzana Camp with a small stream of its own 6.2 miles from the start. Continue hiking 1.2 miles upstream, passing Manzana Narrows Camp, to a junction. Bear left here and undertake a dusty switchbacking climb into the San Rafael Mountains. After 2 miles the route levels out and ascends less steeply as it passes two small meadows strung out along the seasonal tributary. Hurricane Deck comes into view as you top the climb at 4,160 feet and descend easily into the old hunting camp of Happy Hunting Grounds, 3.1 miles from the junction. From here it's an easy descent to White Ledge Camp, 1 mile down the trail on White Ledge Creek. The area gets its name from the white sandstone formations that dominate the landscape of Hurricane Deck.

The following morning, follow the Hurricane Deck Trail (30W14) out of camp on a steep climb up the barren, sparsely chaparraled slopes of the deck. After 2 miles, the trail crests at a saddle and continues its winding up and down way along the top of the ridge for another 4 miles before coming to a junction. There are expansive views to the north of the Sierra Madre Range and also into Sisquoc Canyon. To the south, McKinley, Cachuma, and Figueroa mountains dominate the skyline. At this junction, you leave the deck and travel on a steep switchbacking descent along the Lost Valley Trail (29W14) into Lost Valley Canyon where the trail shortly turns into an old jeep road. Also along here is an unmarked turnoff to Pool Rock and Condor Cave. You will be compensated for the 6.5-mile trek along this road down to Lost Valley Camp by a rest along cool Manzana Creek. While refreshing, you might speculate in your mind's eye about the hardy lives led by the ancient Chumash who would make this and similar journeys as a matter of course. When sufficiently refreshed, complete the remaining mile on the Manzana Trail back to NIRA.

TOPOS: *Bald Mountain, Hurricane Deck, Figueroa Mountain, San Rafael Mountain. W/A*

#53
THE GREAT CIRCLE ROUTE THROUGH
THE SAN RAFAEL
40.6-Mile Loop

Description: Those who savor cool, green canyons, pioneer history, and a lengthy wilderness experience will surely want to set a week more aside some spring to sample the delights of this grand circle excursion. Your route explores in one long loop the heart of the 151,000-acre San Rafael Wilderness, an area especially alive with color and movement in March and April. You will experience the deep and remote Sisquoc Canyon, the unspoiled heart of the wilderness area, where a group of faith healers, often mistakenly called Mormons, settled in the 1880s after a long sojourn from Kansas. The foundations of some of their stone houses and other ruins—bleached fenceposts, rusting pipes, scattered strands of decaying barbed wire—dot the landscape here, and you will find their individual stories thoroughly recounted in Trip #55. You will also investigate the drainage of Manzana Creek, a beautiful free-flowing stream, whose banks play host to many of the numerous wildflower species of the region. Allow at least five complete days for this wilderness trek, with overnight stops at Manzana Narrows, South Fork, Abel Canyon, and Manzana Schoolhouse trail camps.

Driving: NIRA Roadhead.

Directions: Cross the creek and hike upstream along the Manzana Trail (30W13) into the San Rafael Wilderness. You cross over a low ridge guarded by digger pines and then pass Lost Valley Camp, an easy mile away. The Lost Valley Trail to the left here is part of the White Ledge Loop covered in Trip #52 and is also the way to the Indian sites at Pool Rock and Condor Cave.

Continuing southeast along rushing Manzana Creek on a well-graded trail, you pass a junction with the indistinct spur leading in 2.4 miles to Fish Creek Camp on an exposed flat on the other side of Manzana Creek. Phlox, lupine, and poppy decorate the trailside as you descend to a crossing and continue along the opposite bank. After crossing several tributary streams, you reach oak- and manzanita-shaded Manzana Camp with a small stream all its own in 2.9 miles. Upstream a short 0.8 miles away, is Manzana Narrows Camp, a good first night's stop. Fishing here is reasonably good and the finest swimming hole on Manzana Creek is located just downstream.

An early start is recommended the following morning, for some dry, dusty slopes lie ahead. Continue upstream on the Manzana Trail for 0.4 miles to a junction. The right spur here heads 2.5 hard miles to Bigcone Spruce Camp, but your route bears left and undertakes a switchbacking climb into the San Rafael Mountains. After about 2 miles, the route ascends less steeply and passes two potreros strung out along a seasonal stream. The weathered sandstone formations that constitute Hurricane Deck come into view when you top your climb at 4,160 feet and descend easily into the old hunting camp of Happy Hunting Grounds, 3.5 miles beyond the Narrows. It is an easy descent from the camp down to a creek crossing, from which you traverse a chaparraled slope 1 mile to White Ledge Camp at the junction with the Hurricane Deck Trail. This is a good lunch stop and also a fine lookout. The camp gets its name from the huge white sandstone formations that dominate the landscape of Hurricane Deck. Your rest over, follow the creek down from camp, ascend briefly, then continue along the Manzana Trail on a sometimes switchbacking descent 2 miles to Lonnie Davis Camp, and old cow and fishing camp on the South Fork of the Sisquoc River. You may wish to overnight here or, if you still have the energy, continue down to South Fork Camp, an easy 0.8 mile hike through a forest of cottonwoods and sycamores. This camp is located at the junction of the Sisquoc and Manzana trails.

On your third hiking day head northwest downstream along the Sisquoc Trail (27W07). You cross the wide stream below camp and travel along the river's north bank for about 2 miles, passing a junction with the Sweetwater Trail (27W06), which climbs steeply up to Salisbury Potrero. You cross the river again, hike through a meadow, and ford several times above and below the points where the river channel enters a narrows. Your 4 miles of meandering downstream from the South Fork finally rewards you with Sycamore Camp shaded by live oaks with nary a sycamore in sight. Just downstream on a flat there is a junction with the Jackson Trail (27W05), which climbs up to the top of the Sierra Madres. This junction marks the site of the original Sycamore Camp, actually part of the Ed Montgomery Homestead, where indeed an old sycamore once stood.

Hike 3 miles farther down the Sisquoc where cottonwoods, alders, and live oaks intersperse with brush and grasses. You walk through several more fords of the river, pass Big Bend Canyon, descend to small Cliff Camp, and hike 1 mile farther to Abel Canyon Camp, deeply shaded by live oaks on a large flat. Tasty miner's lettuce grows in the area. This spot, with good fishing and swimming holes nearby, makes for a restful night's stop after a long day on the trail.

From Abel Canyon Camp, day four of your trek follows the Sisquoc streambed down the canyon, and the ruins of the 1880s settlement begin to occasionally appear in the brush. Most noticeable are those you pass near Oak and Wellman Canyons during the 4-mile hike to streamside Mormon Camp. Beyond Mormon, the trail is badly washed out and the 2.2-mile hike to Water Canyon Camp must be negotiated in the sandy, wide wash of the streambed. Additional ruins—piles of stone, strands of wire, a rusting plowshare—appear along the dusty trail the remaining 4.3 miles to Manzana Schoolhouse. Grazing cattle, part of the U.S.F.S. Multiple Use Program, are frequently encountered. As you near 2,436-foot Wheat Peak, cross the river and follow the now distinct trail through the grassy riverside potreros to the large camp at Manzana Schoolhouse at the confluence of the Sisquoc River and Manzana Creek. I suggest spending your fourth night here.

At the campsite, you regain the Manzana Trail (30W13) and hike on upstream, your pace slowed by numerous stream crossings. In 2 miles you pass the Dabney Cabin, an old recreational use lot now leased by the Sierra Club. You continue up the Manzana for 3 miles through meadowlands and pass more vestiges of homesteading to reach Coldwater Camp on the north bank of the Manzana. The trail then climbs briefly from the camp and travels mostly along the creek to Potrero Camp, reached in 1.8 miles. From Potrero, continue the remaining mile to the Sunset Valley Road and the end of your loop trip at NIRA Roadhead.

TOPOS: *Bald Mountain, Figueroa Mountain, San Rafael Mountain, Zaca Lake, Hurricane Deck.* F/C.

#54
A CHUMASH CAMPSITE HIGH IN THE SIERRA MADRE
16.4-Mile Loop

Description: Although the Chumash Indians of the Santa Barbara area located their permanent villages in valleys and at canyon mouths along the coast, during spring and fall they ventured high into the backcountry to forage. The men hunted deer and bear; the women gathered acorns, bulbs, tubers, and herbs. They also traveled through the backcountry along established routes to trade with the Indians of the southern San Joaquin Valley, distant cousins called the Yokuts. But while in the mountains, the family groups would encamp year after year in places which provided both good forage and ample water, often near a cave where medicine men worked their magic.

One such place was set high in the Sierra Madre Range. It is today known for its unusual rock pictographs, its many springs, and its beautiful location on a wide grassy meadow. On this two-day backpack trip, you'll explore the Sierra Madre on a climb up Lion Canyon to Painted Rock. Then, after a night at the campsite, you will complete a loop across the top of the range and descend down Newsome Canyon.

Driving: Lion Spring Roadhead.

Directions: From the parking area, walk back down to a junction and turn left up the remainder of Perkins Road (26W01). You soon pass a locked gate, the Johnson Ranch, and an abandoned phosphate mine before entering National Forest Land. At 1.2 miles from the start, you come to a junction. Bear right here onto the Rocky Ridge Trail (27W04). From here it's 5 long miles to Painted Rock. The trail follows the creek up Lion Canyon for half that distance, passing two seasonal springs. It then switchbacks steeply up through the chaparral with great views of the Cuyama Valley before topping the ridge and dropping gently down to Montgomery Potrero at the camp. There are reliable springs around the perimeter of this meadow. Your topo map will help you find them.

You will have no difficulty enjoying the rest of your day at Painted Rock. In springtime the wildflower displays are exceptional. There are shallow caves to explore, grinding holes at which to wonder, pictographs to mystify, mudlark nests to examine. A mystical air seems to shroud the whole place. Above all, please respect the archaeological significance of Painted Rock.

The second day of your trek is long in terms of mileage, but the going is generally easy. From the camp, head east along the Sierra Madre Fire Road (32S13) as it climbs gently along the top of the range. There are great views down to the Sisquoc River and the San Rafael Wilderness and north to the arid Carizzo Plain. Three miles on you'll pass a junction with the Sweetwater Trail on the right and a half-mile later with the Newsome Trail (27W01) to Salisbury Potrero. Bear left onto the latter, and follow it around the edge of the meadow. Although the Forest Service shows a trail camp here, there isn't one, only a battered line cabin and an old windmill.

Continue on the Bull Ridge Trail (26W01), an old jeep road, at the northern edge of Salisbury Potrero, climb over a hump, around Hill 4580, and you're on your way home. The trail follows the top of Bull Ridge through heavy chaparral, then descends more steeply via some switchbacks to the bottom of Newsome Canyon 3.5 miles beyond Salisbury. Hike easily downhill along the intermittent stream past Lower Newsome Spring another 2 miles to intersect Old Perkins Road again. Bear right and walk the remaining distance to the car.

Those who might consider this last day's march of 10.2 miles a bit too much could turn this into a three-day trip, making a dry bivouac at Salisbury. Either way, pack along plenty of water: There are no convenient reliable sources beyond Painted Rock.

TOPOS: *Hurricane Deck, Salisbury Potrero, New Cuyama.*

#55
DOWN THE HISTORIC SISQUOC TRAIL
33.8 Miles One Way

Description: With the passage of the Homestead Act in 1862, Congress made it practicable for any pioneer to own 160 acres of government-held land. All he had to do was reside on the plot, make suitable improvements to "prove his claim," and after five years he took title to the property. Initially, there were few takers in Santa Barbara County. The Civil War provided a major diversion of nearly everyone's attention, and the focus of most California settlers at that time was on the gold fields and rich farmland to the north.

Following the years of Reconstruction, the momentum of westward migration picked up, and miners from the played-out placer deposits in the Sierra began to move south. There was a new interest in settling the Santa Barbara Backcountry. Some of these old timers like Old Marlowe and Carlos Flores, were loners, solitary fellows who settled in on small potreros, built rustic cabins, planted orchards and vegetable gardens and enjoyed comfortable lives in the empty backcountry. Others, like Fred Forbush and Russell Cottam, were city folk who used their remote mountain cabins as weekend base camps for hunting and fishing trips. Still others were ranchers, like the Reyes and McPherson families, who ran vast herds of cattle out across the Cuyama Valley and over the Sierra Madre. Yet there was another group, a band of religious fundamentalists, we'd call them a "cult" today, who came from the east to settle in the remote Sisquoc Valley. They were led by a fiery man full of God's holy zeal, a man with the unlikely name of Hiram Preservéd Wheat.

Hiram was born in Baring County, Kentucky, in 1830. As a young man he moved to Potowatone, Kansas, where he married and founded his church. His beliefs revolved around the ancient ritual of the laying on of hands and also followed a strict dietary regimen—pork, all animal fats, and milk products were strictly taboo. Perhaps because of their strict diet this group has often been mistakenly referred to as a Mormon party, but they were nothing of the sort.

In the middle 1880s, Hiram's band set out one by one for California. Arriving in the Sisquoc Valley, Wheat homesteaded a claim on

Hiram Preservéd Wheat led a group of faith healers into the Sisquoc Valley at the turn of the century. (BLAKLEY ARCHIVES)

a mesa at the confluence of the Sisquoc River and Manzana Creek. He built a house, and his daughters intermarried with neighboring settlers as they arrived. Eventually, Hiram came to control most of the area. But less than 20 years after they arrived in the valley, things began to sour for the Wheat party and the other settlers. Years of heavy rains were followed by years of draught; those periods between 1894 and 1908 were the worst. In that period, so little precipitation fell that the surviving cattle had to be driven into the high mountains for the then sparse grass. Then, in 1898, the Forest Reserve was established, effectively putting an end to any further homesteading in the canyon. The killing blow came when the owners of the Sisquoc Ranch at the mouth of the canyon closed the main wagon road across their land. With no way to get their meager crops to market, many of the settlers either reconveyed their land or sold out. By 1902, only two families remained. Even Hiram Wheat had left, headed to Oceano in search of new disciples.

It's been nearly a century since these folks scratched out a rugged life in the Sisquoc Canyon, yet some fascinating ruins remain. You will come across many of them—rusting barbed wire, old rock chimneys, collapsed cabins, even a dilapidated one-room schoolhouse—as you explore this portion of the San Rafael Wilderness in the footsteps of the pioneers. Although requiring a long car shuttle, this trip has the unique advantage of taking your party through the heart of the wilderness in a relatively short period of time. Your trek will first follow along the summit of the Sierra Madre Mountains to mysterious Painted Rock. You will then descend into the historic canyon of the Sisquoc and follow the wide river to Manzana Creek. You will then complete your backpack by climbing out of the wilderness and descending to Zaca Lake, the only natural lake in this backcountry. I suggest trying this route in the springtime and allowing a minimum of four full days with camps at Painted Rock, Abel Canyon, and Manzana Schoolhouse.

Driving: Start at McPherson Roadhead; end at Zaca Lake.

Directions: Your hike begins as an easy all-day walk along the closed Sierra Madre Road (32S13) from McPherson Roadhead for 7 miles to Painted Rock Camp. Along the way you will enjoy views of Hurricane Deck, into the Sisquoc Canyon, and out to the Cuyama Badlands. On a clear day you will be able to see all the way northeast to the southern Sierra Nevada. Plan to stay your first night at Painted Rock, site of a primitive Chumash encampment. Pictographs dot the inside walls of the shallow sandstone caves here. Clear water is available from nearby Montgomery Spring. The meadow near camp boasts a magnificent gold- and blue-hued wildflower display in the spring. It was named for an old-timer named Josiah Montgomery who built an adobe nearby and ran cattle up on these high potreros.

The following morning, walk back to the spring and continue over a low ridge on the overgrown road that is the Jackson Trail (27W05). This road was also named for another old-timer who ran cattle in the area. It soon narrows to a footpath as it descends steeply at times through old growth chaparral. Finally, 5.5 knee-rattling miles later, you reach the Sisquoc Trail (30W12) at the river. You are standing on the site of the old Ed Montgomery Homestead. Ed was the son of Josiah and his was the last homestead this far upcanyon. Beyond this point the old wagon road ended at a narrows beyond which the wagons could not pass. If you are completely out of energy, you can rest up over-night at Sycamore Camp, 0.2 miles upstream, but I suggest you con-sider continuing on before making camp. At the aforementioned junction turn right and follow the Sisquoc Trail downstream an addi-tional 4 relatively easy miles to Abel Canyon Camp. This is the site of yet another homestead founded by Henry Abel before the turn of the century. Henry was an Englishman, and employed himself as a harness and saddle maker. Although he eventually moved back to Santa Maria, his son, Henry Jr., became one of the first local game wardens. I suggest you stop here for the evening under a canopy of live oaks.

Day three of your route continues down the Sisquoc Trail where you encounter still more ruins of pioneer settlements. There are re-mains of the Miller Homestead in the form of an old stock fence and house foundation near Miller Canyon Camp, and still more beyond the mouth of Oak Canyon. Just before reaching Mormon Camp you will come across the old Willman settlement near the mouth of Wellman Canyon. The Willmans were a German family and, with ex-tensive fruit orchards, cattle, and a large vegetable garden, were among the most prosperous settlers in the canyon. Additional remains of this settlement will be found along the remaining 2.2-mile trail to Water Canyon Camp.

John Twichell homesteaded the mesa just south of Water Canyon, and farther along, during the remaining 4.3 miles to Manzana Schoolhouse Camp you will find the site of William Spitler's 1885 claim, where an old stone chimney presides over a now dead orchard.

Manzana Schoolhouse as it appeared in 1956. (BLAKLEY ARCHIVES)
Falls Creek Falls in the San Rafael Wilderness.
(U.S. FOREST SERVICE)

Beyond there, following the southern shore of the Sisquoc River, you enter Hiram Wheat's territory. The remains of Wheat's old home can be located on top of Wheat Mesa on the north bank of the river where there is a rock chimney on the edge of a dump with purple glass and rusted tin cans. To the east of that same mesa is the Wells Homestead, where once stood a house and a barn. Now you will find only a foundation and collapsing chimney. Plan to spend the remainder of this day camped at Manzana Schoolhouse, where you can explore these relics into the past and speculate on the hearty lives of these pioneers who journeyed from their faraway home in Kansas to settle here in the Sisquoc Canyon of Santa Barbara County. Near camp is the still-standing Manzana Schoolhouse built of timbers in 1893 to educate the children of the settlers. It is now a Santa Barbara County historical landmark. Close by stood a small post office built in 1896. It was active for only five months until the post office department discovered that the postman could neither read nor write. The local postman was Hiram Wheat.

Your fourth and final day on the trail is also your shortest. From Manzana Schoolhouse, travel easily upstream on the Manzana Trail

(30W13) through several stream crossings. On the way you pass the remains of Joseph Adkins' small homestead; he was married to one of Wheat's daughters. A little farther on is the small home built by Alvis Davis and now occupied by local sculptor, John Cody. It is the only inholding of private land still extant in the San Rafael Wilderness.

Just a short distance beyond is the Dabney Cabin. It was built for Charles Dabney in 1914 on a 99-year recreation lease from the Forest Service. It is currently leased out by a local chapter of the Sierra Club. Shortly after the cabin is a turnoff to the right on a closed jeep road. Follow this retiring road leaving the wilderness area and travel a short way uphill watching for the obvious beginning of the Zaca Trail (30W07) on the left. Hike this steep but shaded trail upwards, crossing the jeep road a number of times, until a saddle is finally reached at the last road crossing, 3 miles beyond Dabney. I suggest stopping for lunch here under the tall pines to enjoy a great view back into the wilderness. From the saddle, continue steeply downhill, still on the Zaca Trail (now numbered 30W09), the remaining 1.8 miles to Zaca Lake and resort, your shuttle point.

TOPOS: *Peak Mountain, Hurricane Deck, Bald Mountain, Zaca Lake.*
W/A

Falls Creek Falls in the San Rafael Wilderness. (U.S. FOREST SERVICE)

VI

THE TRAIL CAMPS

TRAIL CAMPS in the southern Los Padres National Forest are back-country sites provided by the Forest Service for the day and overnight use of hikers. Accessible only by foot or on horseback (a few can be reached by motorcycle and some by mountain bike), they are distinct from CAMPGROUNDS, which can be reached by passenger vehicles and are provided for car campers.

The number of stoves at each camp will give you a good idea of its size. A camp with four stoves, for example, generally has room for four groups of backpackers. Some sites also have tables; the Forest Service, however, is no longer replacing tables as they succumb to use, so you may not find as many as I have listed. Stove and table information is based on 1986 U.S.F.S. inventories.

Most camps are located near reliable water sources—streams or springs. Many are along "seasonal" or "intermittent" streams that run only during the wet months. Be aware, though, that even the most reliable creek may cease to flow in an unusually dry year. Without exception, the best time to hike in the Santa Barbara Backcountry is during spring and late fall.

The directions I have provided include everything you need to know to get to each camp. The altitude of each camp is given in parentheses following its name. ONE-WAY mileage from the roadhead to each camp follows the elevation, also in parentheses. For driving directions to the roadhead named for each camp, consult the "Roadheads" chapter.

Following each write-up is a list of the U.S. geological Survey maps that cover the route to each camp. All U.S.G.S. maps noted are in the 7.5-minute series and are available at Southern California mountain and map shops. "F/C" indicates that the trail camp is located in the traditional summer fire closure area. "W/A" means the camp is in a designated wilderness.

The trail camps in this chapter are listed alphabetically for your convenience. All the latest information is provided. I have included directions to each camp from the nearest roadhead and include directions to the newest camps the Forest Service has constructed. A few camps are no longer maintained, but since they still appear on many maps, I have included them in the listing.

I neither have nor would want to include every possible route to every possible destination in this guidebook. A large part of the adventure and enjoyment of backcountry traveling, after all, comes from finding your own way, planning your own route, making your own discoveries. Rather, this chapter is provided to give you an overview of specific campsites in this vast backcountry area. Use it to plan your own special experience. Remember that new changes in Forest Service policy no longer require that you camp at these designated sites. The new Remote Area Camping Policy allows backcountry users to bivouac outside established camps (except in the San Rafael and Dick Smith wilderness areas) as long as certain regulations are observed. The nearest district ranger office can fill you in. See Chapter 1 for details on campfire permits.

ABEL CANYON (1,750')(16.5) Situated on the Sisquoc Trail in the center of the San Rafael Wilderness, this camp has two stoves and a reliable water supply from the river. There are excellent fishing and swimming holes at Abel, which was named for a Santa Maria family that used the site as a hunting outpost around the turn of the century.

From McPherson Roadhead follow the Sierra Madre Road (32S13) an easy 7 miles southeast to Painted Rock. Descend a steep 5.5 miles on the Jackson Trail (27W05) to the Sisquoc River. Travel down the canyon on the Sisquoc Trail (30W12) 4 miles past Cliff Camp to Abel Canyon. This route is covered in detail under "Down the Historic Sisquoc Trail," Trip #55.
TOPOS: *Hurricane Deck, Peak Mountain.* W/A

ALDER CREEK (Santa Barbara County)(2,600')(2.9) Alder Camp is set on the southern forested slope of Upper Santa Ynez Canyon.

It was developed during the depression by the C.C.C. but has since fallen into disuse. One battered table and a fire ring are all you will find here now. Stream water is reliable.

From Juncal Roadhead, follow the Santa Ynez Fire Road (5N13) east past the locked gate and proceed on a gradual climb up to and around Juncal Dam. About halfway along Jameson Lake, watch on the right for a flume that diverts the flow from Alder Creek into the reservoir. Leave the road here and descend to the flume to pick up the Franklin Trail (25W09). Follow this pathway moderately up the canyon to reach the shady camp in less than a mile.

TOPOS: *Carpinteria, White Ledge Peak*

ALDER CREEK (Ventura County)(2,520′)(6.2) On an isolated stream near the boundary of the Sespe Condor Sanctuary, this camp is ideal for a quiet weekend of reflection. There are two stoves here, but water is only certain during the wet months. Firearms are prohibited in the area.

From Dough Flat Roadhead, hike up closed Fire Road 6N16, staying left at a "Y," 3 miles to Cow Springs Camp. Then follow the Alder Creek Connector Trail (20W11) on a level, then downhill, trek, which becomes steep at times, past Dripping Springs to a trail junction in 2.6 miles. Bear left and continue an easy 0.6 miles on the Alder Creek Trail (20W13) downstream to the camp.

TOPO: *Devils Heart Peak*

ALEJANDRO (1,640′(3.7) Named for Alejandro Ontiveras, son of the Mexican family that bought the Tepesquet land grant in Santa Barbara County, this infrequently visited camp has two stoves, two tables, and the solitude of a quiet remote canyon. This site is shaded by numerous live oaks.

From the Colson Roadhead, follow the Alejandro Canyon Trail (31W15) on a steep switchbacking climb through chaparral 0.5 miles to a ridgetop where is the great view of nearby Zaca Peak. Bear left at the junction at the top of a ridge and follow the Alejandro Trail easily downstream into the canyon 3 miles. The little camp is located along a seasonal stream.

TOPO: *Tepesquet Canyon*

ANT (2,700′)(6.1) Arranged on the level floor of Agua Blanca Canyon directly below the brooding hulk of Cobblestone Mountain, this trail camp can serve as a fine base for a weekend exploration of this remote canyon on the northern fringe of the Sespe Condor Sanctuary. Upstream is remote Saddle Skirt Camp. Downstream, the site of Tin Can Cabin. Firearms are prohibited in this area. There are two stoves and one table here.

From Dough Flat Roadhead, continue up closed Fire Road 6N16 on a moderate grade. At 2.5 miles bear right at the "Y" to Bucksnort Springs and continue northeast on this spur road a short distance to a sign directing you toward the Agua Blanca Trail. Stay on the dirt road, which climbs to a saddle and trail register. Then descend by the Bucksnort Trail (19W18), switchbacking at times, on a moderate hike to the oak-shaded camp, 3.6 miles beyond Bucksnort. There did seem to be an inordinate number of ants at Ant Camp.
TOPO: *Devils Heart Peak.* F/C

BALLARD (2,080′)(1.8) Often overlooked because of its seeming inaccessibility, this camp with three stoves and one table nevertheless makes a fine retreat. It is located at the site of an old hunting camp used by William Ballard, a man who built and supervised a Wells Fargo stage depot in the Santa Ynez Valley in the mid-1880s. Water is available from dependable Birabent Creek. There are actually two Ballard Camps, the upper unit I'm describing and a smaller one with a single stove farther downstream.

From Ballard Roadhead hike on down the Birabent Trail (30W10) traveling north across a meadow. Bear northeast and then descend a steep switchbacking 1.8 miles through chaparral to arrive at the small oak-shaded camp along the creek. The trail to the lower unit of the camp heads downstream past the remains of an old frame building and pump station for 0.7 miles to the junction with the Birabent Canyon Trail.
TOPOS: *Zaca Lake, Las Olivos*

BEAR (5,280′)(13.7) Just within the boundary of the San Rafael Wilderness, this site was originally used as a hunting camp by the Hartman Brothers early in this century. It was they who built the large concrete stove, which still survives. The camp suffered severe damage in the flood of 1969 but is still used. The springs that form the headwaters of the Sisquoc River bubble out from the mountain nearby.

From Santa Barbara Canyon Roadhead, follow the closed Santa Barbara Canyon Fire Road (9N11) on a winding uphill ascent to Santa Barbara Potrero in 4.5 miles. Bear left at the "Y" here and continue on the Big Pine Road (9N11) on an easy to moderate grade for 8.4 miles to the junction with the Sisquoc River Trail (27W07) on the right. Follow this switchbacking path downhill to the west for 0.8 miles to the trail camp located at the end of the spur trail to your left.

For another route to Bear Camp, see "The Southern Loop Through The San Rafael," Trip #51.

TOPOS: *Big Pine Mountain, Salisbury Potrero, Fox Mountain, Madulce Peak.* W/A, F/C

BEAR CANYON (1,360′) (3.2) Located in a remote section of the northern Santa Barbara Backcountry, this camp, in a canyon of the same name, sees little use outside of hunting season. Chaparral covers the hillsides, shade is sparse, water unreliable. Only a single stove marks the spot.

From Bear Canyon Roadhead, follow the Bear Canyon Trail (31W05) north upstream. The pathway is in poor shape and there are numerous stream crossings all the way to the camp.

TOPO: *Tepesquet Canyon*

BEARTRAP #1 (5,060′)(5.0) Lodged in a quiet canyon below Reyes Peak, this camp is on the Beartrap–Piedra Blanca Trail. It has two stoves and two tables. Generally reliable Beartrap Creek offers some fair fishing possibilities. This camp was the site of bear-trapping operations in the mid and late nineteenth century by the Reyes family when grizzlies were still abundant in these mountains.

From the Reyes Creek Roadhead follow the Beartrap Trail (32W02) uphill through chaparral. Bear left at a junction with a spur trail coming up from private Scheideck Camp and continue on a moderate ascent with only a few patches of shade provided by stately bigcone spruce sentinels. In 2.5 miles you top a low saddle and descend 1 mile to Upper Reyes Camp. Your route travels briefly upcanyon, then ascends by switchbacks 0.8 miles to the top of the ridge dividing the drainages of Beartrap and Reyes creeks. You descend steeply but easily down into Beartrap Canyon another 0.7 miles to reach the creekside camp shaded by oak and pine.

TOPO: *Reyes Peak*

BIGCONE (1,680′)(3.0) This attractive camp, heavily used because of its easy accessibility, is on Santa Paula Creek where live oaks and bigcone spruce mingle. It has six camp stoves and tables. A hitching post is provided. No firearms are allowed.

From the roadhead at Ferndale Ranch follow the Santa Paula Canyon Trail (21W10) across the ranch easement and continue upstream along Santa Paula Creek on Fire Road 4N03 on an easy grade. After crossing the creek, the wide trail climbs moderately up and around Hill 1989 and then descends easily to the wide shady bench harboring the camp. Ample drinking water is available from Santa Paula Creek, 100 feet and a few switchbacks below. The poor trail out of Bigcone leads upstream to Cross, Cienega, and Bluff camps.

TOPO: *Santa Paula Peak.* F/C

BIGCONE SPRUCE (3,920′)(10.0) Located in the San Rafael Wilderness in a canyon near the headwaters of Manzana Creek on McKinley Mountain, this camp is arranged streamside with two wilderness stoves and a table near a grove of mature bigcone spruce. The last 2.5 miles of the trail to the camp were washed out a few years ago and have not been repaired.

From the NIRA Roadhead follow the Manzana Trail (30W13) 7 miles upstream according to the directions given below for Manzana Narrows Camp. Continue on the Manzana Trail upstream for 0.4 miles to a junction. Bear right here onto Trail 28W07 and boulder hop your way up this side canyon a rough and tiring 2.5 miles to reach Bigcone Spruce. A few remaining vestiges of the trail remain to help you out. Only a poor trail continues up from the camp.

TOPOS: *San Rafael Mountain, Figueroa Mountain, Bald Mountain.* W/A

BIG PINE (6,150′)(14.6) Located a short way off the Buckhorn Road and just within the boundaries of the San Rafael Wilderness, Big Pine is one of the largest and most comfortable camps in the Santa Barbara Backcountry. You'll find six stoves, three tables, and a reliable spring here under the conifers that blanket the slopes of Big Pine and West Big Pine Mountains. The Hartman Brothers from Ventura originally set up an elaborate hunting camp here in the early 1900s. It was not uncommon for them to pack in supplies during the summer using up to 20 mules to provide for their large family. While the men hunted and fished for weeks at a time, a Chinese cook maintained Big Pine as a base camp. Later the C.C.C. used the site as a base of operations during the construction of the Buckhorn Fire Road.

From the Santa Barbara Canyon Roadhead follow the Buckhorn Road (9N11) west 4.5 miles to a junction with the Sierra Madre Road (32S13) at Santa Barbara Potrero. Turn left (south) here and continue along the Buckhorn Road (9N11) on an easy to moderate grade passing junctions with the trails to Madulce, Bill Faris, and Bear Camps. A mile and a half beyond the latter, in the shadow of Big Pine, watch on the right for an unsigned trail that leads down past a large stand of chokecherries a quarter-mile to the camp.

TOPOS: *Big Pine Mountain, Salisbury Potrero, Fox Mountain, Madulce Peak.* F/C, W/A

BILL FARIS (4,200´)(17.8) Named for an outstanding Santa Barbara Boy Scout leader, this camp on spring-fed Alamar Creek features two stoves, a table, and a fine view of Madulce Peak. The area is forested with chaparral. It would not be an understatement to say that Bill Faris (1) is difficult to reach, (2) is in the middle of nowhere, and (3) is only visited by backpackers as part of a long remote trek.

From the roadhead at Mono Dam follow the 10.9-mile route to Lower Alamar Camp as described below. From Lower Alamar, increasingly difficult Trail 25W05 travels north in Alamar Canyon. The trail number changes to 26W05 and a junction is reached in 4.8 miles. Bear left and follow Trail 26W06 the remaining 2 miles to the camp. This is a strenuous hike and definitely not for beginners.

TOPOS: *Madulce Peak, Hildreth Peak.* F/C, W/A

BLUE CANYON (1,710´)(1.3) Called Lower Blue Canyon Camp on some maps, this site was somehow spared the ravages of the 1964 Coyote Fire. The surrounding hillsides, then largely denuded, have recovered. Facilities include two stoves, one rustic table, and a water supply dependable except in dry years. It's a fine hike for a picnic or easy overnight backpack.

From the roadhead near Romero Saddle, simply walk down the hillside from where the sign marks the start of the trail. There really is no trail any more, so just walk under the high tension wires and continue down to the creek. Then turn left (west) and follow the Blue Canyon Trail (26W12) to the camp on a grassy flat, 1.3 miles from the East Camino Cielo Road.

TOPO: *Carpinteria*

BLUE JAY (3,550')(14.2) Anyone who's spent any time camping knows that this campsite is named for those fleet-of-wing robbers who are always on the alert to pluck any unguarded morsel from any hiker's picnic. This small camp with only one stove has its share of jays. It's set on a little flat along Indian Creek near Big Pine Mountain deep in the Dick Smith Wilderness. Oaks and bigcone spruce provide welcome shade. There are wading pools nearby. The camp is not shown on most maps.

From Mono Roadhead, follow the directions given below to Pens Camp. Continue upstream on the Indian Creek Trail (26W08) past Poplar Camp 1.8 miles to Blue Jay. Bluff Camp on the Buckhorn Road is 2.2 miles beyond.

TOPOS: *Little Pine Mountain, Big Pine Mountain, Hildreth Peak, Madulce Peak.* F/C, W/A

BLUFF (Ventura County)(4,000')(9.5) Set below steep red sandstone bluffs near the Sespe Sanctuary's southwest boundary, this camp has two stoves and tables. Water is available all year from a nearby spring. I would suggest this site to those desiring isolation.

From the roadhead in Timber Canyon follow the directions given below to Cienega Camp up, over, and down Santa Paula Ridge (8 miles). From there, follow Trail 21W10 northeast a moderately difficult 1.5 miles up to the camp. This hike is long, hot, and strenuous.

TOPO: *Santa Paula Peak.* F/C

BLUFF (Santa Barbara County)(4,720′)(19.5) Originally used as a base camp for C.C.C. construction crews building the Big Pine Road during the Depression, this camp now lies 5 miles beyond the end of a designated motorcycle route. The way there is dusty and monotonous and also noisy on weekends. The camp, with two stoves and tables, seldom sees hikers. Spring water is provided. Another route to Bluff is described as part of "The Southern Loop Through The San Rafael," Trip #51.

From the roadhead at Upper Oso Campground, walk past the locked gate and follow the Camuesa Fire Road (5N15) past Hidden Potrero to a junction in 4 miles. Bear left onto Fire Road 6N13 and follow it, steeply at times, 5 miles to a junction near Little Pine Mountain. Bear right onto the Big Pine Road (9N11) and continue a winding and moderate 10.5 miles to the camp, off the road near the U.S.F.S. Staion. Be sure to pack along a lot of extra water for this long, dry trek.
TOPOS: *Big Pine Mountain, Little Pine Mountain, San Marcos Pass.*
F/C

BUCK CREEK (3,500′)(3.2) Nestled in a chaparral-covered canyon near Pyramid Lake Reservoir, where bigcone spruce dot the landscape, this camp features a single stove and table. Buck Creek, draining Black and White mountains, provides a dependable water supply. There is also a spring nearby.

From Hardluck Roadhead follow the Buck Creek Trail (18W01) across the creek and then upstream. The trail then climbs up the southern side of the canyon and ascends moderately to reach the camp on a flat in 3.1 miles.
TOPO: *Black Mountain*

CEDAR CREEK (5,050′)(3.1) Situated in a cool, attractive canyon amid pine, spruce, and stream woodland, this little camp has three stoves and two tables. Water is available most of the year from the creek. With little elevation gain involved, this is one of the easiest and most pleasant hikes in the Mount Piños Disctict of the Los Padres National Forest.

From the roadhead at Thorn Meadows, walk up closed Fire Road 22W10 west for 2.5 miles. The road turns to trail at this point and you bear left and travel 0.6 miles to the camp on the south fork of Piru Creek. The trail leading out of camp continues to the Fishbowls and Pine Mountain Lodge.

TOPOS: *San Guillermo, Lockwood Valley*

CHORRO GRANDE SPRING (6,400′)(1.0) Great as a picnic, day hike, or overnight backpack destination not far from the car, this small, secluded camp is on the southern slope of Pine Mountain. Ponderosa pine and white fir carpet the mountainside with their soft needles and provide welcome shade. There is a gushing spring (''chorro'') here, as well as four stoves and a hitching post.

From Pine Mountain Roadhead, just beyond Reyes Peak Campground, follow the signed Chorro Grande trail (23W05) south steeply downhill for 1 mile to the camp. There are two extensive views of the forested slopes of the Sespe watershed to the south.

TOPO: *Reyes Peak*

CIENEGA (3,480′)(6.5) Set near a springy meadow in a deep canyon below Santa Paula Peak, this camp has three stoves. The trail to this spot is unmaintained and in poor shape.

From the Ferndale Ranch Roadhead, follow the Santa Paula Canyon Trail (21W10) across the ranch easement and continue upstream along Santa Paula Creek on Fire Road 4N03. After a stream crossing, the wide trail continues moderately up and around Hill 1989 and descends to Bigcone Camp, 3 miles total. Descend by switchbacks to the creek and ascend up the east fork of Santa Paula Canyon for 3.3 miles on a moderate grade on a poor trail to a junction with the Santa Paula Peak Trail. Bear left and hike 0.2 miles to the camp. The trail leading out of camp climbs to Bluff Camp near the Condor Sanctuary.

TOPO: *Santa Paula Peak.* F/C

CLIFF (1,800′)(15.5) Cliff Camp is situated beneath an imposing promontory in Sisquoc Canyon. It has two wilderness stoves and a dependable water supply. Since it's a new trail camp, it does not appear on many older maps. Cliff is part of ''Down The Historic Sisquoc,'' Trip #55.

From McPherson Roadhead follow the instructions provided below to Sycamore Camp (12.5 miles). From the junction just below the camp turn right and travel along the Sisquoc Trail (30W12) downstream past several fine swimming and fishing holes 3 miles to Cliff Camp.
TOPOS: *Hurricane Deck, Salisbury Potrero, Peak Mountain.* W/A

COCHE (3,320 ')(17.3) Named for the wild pigs that are said to have once inhabited this corner of the San Rafael Wilderness, this camp on dependable Coche Creek offers two stoves.

From the roadhead at Upper Oso Campground follow the detailed directions given below for 11.5 tiring miles to Santa Cruz Camp. From that streamside camp follow the Santa Cruz Trail (27W09) northwest up Black Canyon, then veer off and climb moderately 1.2 miles and 800 feet to the ridge that marks the boundary for the wilderness area. Be sure to stay right at a junction with a northwest spur trail to Santa Cruz Peak. From the ridge, it is an easy 1.6-mile descent down to Flores Camp on the west fork of Santa Cruz Creek.

Leaving Flores, follow the west fork upstream to a trail junction. You bear right, cross over a low hill, and join Coche Creek. Follow it upstream through a half-dozen crossings 3 miles to Coche Camp. There is a marked junction with the Grapevine Trail (27W10) just below camp.
TOPOS: *Big Pine Mountain, San Rafael Mountain, Little Pine Mountain, San Marcos Pass.* F/C, W/A.

COLDWATER (1,640 ')(2.8) Although destroyed by the flood of 1969, this popular wilderness trail camp on Manzana Creek with four stoves has been rebuilt and relocated downstream 2 miles from its former location. The hike is fairly easy and studded with several species of wildflowers in spring. The lupine and shooting star displays are particularly beautiful. I highly recommend it.

From the NIRA Roadhead, walk back along the Sunset Valley Road a short distance to recross the creek. The Manzana Trail (30W13), marked by a sign and a register, takes off from here and winds above Manzana Creek to descend in 1 mile at Potrero Camp. From there continue downstream on the Manzana Trail an easy 1.8 miles to Coldwater, located on a streamside meadow shaded by digger pines, with a reliable water supply.

TOPO: *Bald Mountain.* W/A

COTTAM (1,550')(2.4) This camp in Blue Canyon, also known as Lower Blue Canyon Camp, has three stoves and two tables with a fairly reliable water supply. It's just a short way down from East Camino Cielo and is a great destination for a picnic or a day hike. The camp is at the site of a cabin built by Russell Cottam under a special use permit issued by the Forest Service near the turn of the century.

From Romero Saddle Roadhead simply walk down the hillside from where the sign marks the start of the Romero Trail (26W14). After you pass under the high tension wires, continue down to the creek. Then turn left (west) and follow the Blue Canyon Trail (26W12) to Blue Canyon Camp, 1.3 miles from the start. Continue easily down the Blue Canyon Trail the remaining 1.5 miles to Cottam Camp located near the confluence of Forbush and Blue canyons.

TOPO: *Carpinteria*

COTTONWOOD (3,200')(19.2) On a flat beside the reliable Sisquoc River, this wilderness camp with three stoves was named for the stately cottonwood trees that border the stream in the area. Nearby grasslands are abundant with spring wildflowers. Rattlesnake Falls is also close by.

From Lion Spring Roadhead follow the Bull Ridge Fire Road and Trail (26W01) moderately uphill 6.8 miles to Salisbury Potrero. Turn left onto the Sierra Madre Fire Road (32S13) and hike southeast an easy winding 6 miles to Santa Barbara Potrero. Here you pick up the brushy Judell Canyon Trail (25W05) and moderately descend 5 miles to Heath Camp on the Sisquoc River. Travel west along the Sisquoc Trail (27W07) an easy 1.4 miles to Cottonwood Camp.

TOPOS: *Big Pine Mountain, Hurricane Deck, Salisbury Potrero.* F/C, W/A

COVE (1,730')(8.2) This secluded and almost-forgotten site is on a bend of Agua Blanca Creek about midway between Log Cabin and Ant camps. Because the access trail is no longer maintained, few hikers venture this far into the backcountry above Lake Piru. A strong hiker can easily follow the streambed when necessary, picking up segments of the old trail as they appear, and make it into camp in about five hours. The site offers two stoves, a hitching post, and a feeling of total remoteness.

From the roadhead at Blue Point Campground, follow the detailed instructions below to Log Cabin Camp (4.5 miles). Continue upstream on a boulder-hopping hike in the streambed and along what's left of the Agua Blanca Trail (19W10). You will reach the camp 3.7 miles after Log Cabin. Beyond here, the few vestiges of the Agua Blanca Trail climb above the Big Narrows and descend to Ant Camp in a very difficult 6.2 miles. Firearms are prohibited.
TOPO: *Cobblestone Mountain.* F/C

COW SPRING (3,520′)(3.0) Formerly a car campground, this site with six stoves and tables was closed to vehicular traffic in 1973 due to repeated vandalism and its close proximity to the Sespe Sanctuary. Cow Spring is one of the best observation points in the National Forest from which to watch for the soaring flights of the few remaining California condors. There is no water here.

From the roadhead at Dough Flat, travel on Fire Road 6N16 uphill on a fairly easy grade. Stay left at a "Y" and you'll reach the camp on a wide, open flat 3 miles from the start. The Alder Creek Connector Trail (20W11) begins here at Cow Spring and descends to Alder Creek and Indian Cave camps.
TOPO: *Devils Heart Peak*

CROSS (1,820′)(3.5) Named for a Byzantine cross once sculpted on a nearby boulder, this creekside camp in Santa Paula Canyon has five campsites. It's a popular spot and rightly so. Bigcone spruce shade the area. There are several spectacular falls here as Santa Paula Creek cascades down to join its east fork. And the swift flowing stream has carved many large swimming holes from the soft sandstone. With several flat open areas for sunbathing, skinnydipping is not uncommon. A word of caution to swimmers: the creek flows deceptively swift and deep through here. There have been numerous injuries in recent years. Exercise proper caution.

From the roadhead at the Ferndale Ranch, follow the above directions 3 miles to Bigcone Camp. Descend 0.1 miles to the east fork of Santa Paula Creek. Cross the creek, pick up the trail, bear left and continue uphill 0.4 miles to the small streamside camp. Firearms are prohibited in this area.

TOPO: *Santa Paula Peak.* F/C

CUCHUDAS (1,840′)(22.0) Because public access is denied across the Goodchild Ranch property, the logical roadhead for this camp, the only way to get here is by a tortuous brushed-over route out of Manzana Schoolhouse. The camp is located on the south fork of La Brea Creek. It has two stoves, which have likely seen little use in recent years.

From the NIRA Roadhead, follow the Manzana Trail (30W13) 7.8 miles to Manzana Schoolhouse. Turn northwest onto the Sisquoc Trail (30W12) and continue up Horse Canyon past Sluice Box Camp on a poor trail. What's left of the path climbs up out of the canyon and crosses a ridge to seasonable La Brea Creek. Descend along the creek to the site of the camp near the mouth of Owl Canyon.

TOPOS: *Zaca Lake, Bald Mountain, Bates Canyon, Manzanita Mountain*

DEAL JUNCTION (3,700′)(1.4) This site with two stoves was built in the early 1940s by uranium prospectors at the confluence of Rancho Nuevo Creek and Deal Canyon.

From the Rancho Nuevo Roadhead follow the Rancho Nuevo Trail (24W03) upstream past the register and mineral spring and through several stream crossings to reach the camp among chaparral in an easy 1.4 miles. The Deal Canyon Trail travels south from here to Mine Camp. The Rancho Nuevo Trail continues to Upper Rancho Neuvo Camp. Water is seasonally available.

TOPO *Rancho Nuevo Creek.* W/A

DON VICTOR (3,440′)(9.5) The small valley in which this camp is nestled is near the old homestead site of Don Victor, a Basque tuberculosis sufferer who exiled himself to this area in the early 1900s to spend his remaining months of life. He planted vegetables, built pens and corrals for his sheep, and led a long though isolated life in this healthy dry climate. Unfortunately, he ended up drowning in the Ventura River. There are no facilities located at this site any longer, and the route to this camp is long, difficult, and generally washed out. I recommend only seasoned backpackers in good condition attempt the trek to Don Victor.

From the roadhead at Pine Mountain Summit, follow Fire Road 6N03 for 4.5 miles to Potrero Seco Camp. The trail beyond Potrero Seco is gone, and folks who visit Don Victor merely follow the old battered jeep road down the ridge to the northwest.

TOPOS: *Madulce Peak, Rancho Nuevo Creek.* F/C, W/A

DUTCH OVEN (3,720′)(8.5) Dutch Oven is an old campsite located on reliable Alamar Creek that has been used since ancient times. Nearby was the Chumash village of Castiec, and Spanish and Anglos alike were known to have stayed here at this spot, a day's ride between the coast and the Central Valley. It is set below impressive Malduce Peak (6,541 feet) and gets its name from an old dutch oven left here by the Cord brothers, who used the site as a hunting camp. The camp has only a single stove.

From the Santa Barbara Canyon Roadhead hike easily up the Santa Barbara Canyon Trail (25W02) through numerous stream crossings on an old jeep road. Five miles from the start, the trail heads south up a tributary stream, tops a rise, and descends to Madulce Camp and Cabin. Bear east here onto the Mono-Alamar Trail (26W20) to climb out of Pine Canyon and over the Puerto Suela on a shoulder of Madulce Peak. You then descend into Alamar Canyon to reach the camp at a junction with the trail to Bill Faris Camp.

TOPOS: *Fox Mountain, Madulce Peak.* F/C, W/A

EAST FORK LION (3,440′)(2.4) Situated on a large level flat below a series of cascades, this site offers three stoves with plenty of room for large groups. It's often used by Boy and Girl Scout Troops because of its easy access. Water is generally dependable and may be sought out in the upstream narrows in dry months. The lingering damage in the area is the result of the Bear Fire of 1971.

From Middle Lion Roadhead hike along the well-marked Topatopa Trail (22W06) two miles up Lion Canyon to Four Points Trail Junction. The spur to the right travels to West Fork Lion Camp, and the path straight ahead climbs up to Topatopa Ridge. Your route bears to the left, travels across a sandy flat shaded by bigcone spruce, and reaches camp in 0.4 miles.

TOPO: *Lion Canyon*

ELLIS APIARY (1,240′)(2.5) An old, dry, and dusty camp, Ellis was once the site of a small commercial beehive operation. Today there are only two stoves beneath the live oaks on reliable Piru Creek. Water should be purified before drinking.

From the roadhead at Blue Point Campground, walk upstream to a crossing. Pass through the locked gate and continue up the road past the property of the Whitaker Ranch. When the road reaches Agua Blanca Creek, cross it, then bear right and travel back to Piru Creek. From here, the trail is almost completely washed out. Simply walk up the Piru streambed 1.8 miles to the camp. Along the way you will pass many abscesses on the canyon wall caused by erosion of the sedimentary rock. Also visible are the tailings of an old hydraulic gold-mining operation. As the price of gold has climbed, weekend prospectors have become more common along the Piru. The trail beyond Ellis is no longer maintained and is in very bad shape. The route to Ellis follows the abandoned Cobblestone Trail (18W03).

TOPO: *Cobblestone Mountain.* F/C

FISHBOWLS (5,200′)(5.6) Lodged near the headwaters of Piru Creek, this camp with two stoves and tables is named for a series of deep potholes formed by the erosive action of water in the sedimentary rock. Fishing is fair and the water reliable along the Piru. The Fishbowls are fine for swimming.

From the roadhead at Thorn Meadows follow closed Fire Road 22W10 for 2.5 miles west along the south fork of Piru Creek. The road turns to trail at this point and you beat 0.6 miles left to reach streamside Cedar Creek Camp. From here the Fishbowls Trail (22W10) ascends a ridge on a moderate climb to a junction. To the left, Trail 22W10 goes to Pine Mountain Lodge, but your route turns right, still

on the Fishbowls Trail (22W05), levels off briefly, then descends to a small draw. The trail ascends briefly then drops down to cross Piru Creek, which you follow downstream to the camp in a cool cedar and pine-shaded canyon 2.5 miles from Cedar Creek. For a description of a two-day loop trip to Fishbowls, see Trip #37.
TOPOS: *San Guillermo, Lockwood Valley.*

FISH CREEK (2,000′)(2.9) On a grassy flat at the confluence of Fish and Manzana creeks, this wilderness camp, destroyed in the flood of 1969, has been relocated a quarter-mile southeast of the location shown on the topo map. This was once a prime trout fishing area and anglers still have some luck in season. There is one wilderness stove as well as reliable water here.

From NIRA Roadhead follow the Manzana Trail (30W13) east into the San Rafael Wilderness. You pass Lost Valley Camp and Trail (29W14) in 1 mile, and continue on the easy Manzana Trail for another 1.6 miles. Watch to the right for the camp across the stream. The area has a lot of spring wildflowers—especially California poppy, wild hyacinth, chia, and lupine—but the camp is exposed, overused, and not terribly attractive.
TOPO: *Bald Mountain.* W/A

FLORES FLAT (2,400′)(14.3) According to local legend, Carlos Flores, a turn-of-the-century Mexican vaquero, happened upon the meadow now named for him, fell in love with it, and decided to build a cabin. Coming from a farm background, he devised an ingenious system of canals to irrigate his field, where he raised such crops as corn and watermelon. He even kept a few head of cattle to tide him over. Today the homestead is gone, but the beautiful potrero that so enticed Flores remains virtually unchanged and is the location of this attractive camp. The National Forest provides one stove and two tables at this site.

From the Upper Oso Roadhead follow the detailed directions provided below to Santa Cruz Camp (11.5 miles), the southern gateway to the San Rafael Wilderness. From here follow the Santa Cruz Trail (27W09) northwest up Black Canyon, then veer off and complete the 1.2-mile climb to the top of the ridge that marks the wilderness bound-

ary. Stay right here at a junction of a spur trail to Santa Cruz Peak and descend an easy 1.6 miles into Flores Camp on the south fork of Santa Cruz Creek.
TOPOS: *San Rafael Mountain, Little Pine Mountain, San Marcos Pass.* F/C, W/A

FORBUSH FLAT (2,000′)(1.7) Long the home of Fred Forbush, another turn-of-the-century homesteader, this flat still hosts some of his apple and olive trees and grapevines. There are even remnants of the Forbush Cabin dating back to 1910. Shaded by large live oaks, it makes a fine stop for a picnic or overnight weekend hike. There are four stoves and two tables at this location.

From Cold Spring Saddle Roadhead, follow the Cold Springs Trail (26W10) downhill for 1.7 miles to the campsite near a creek and spring at a junction with the Forbush Canyon Trail.
TOPO: *Santa Barbara*

GRIDLEY SPRINGS (2,560′) (2.5) Nestled in a small shallow bend in a fire road on the slopes of Nordhoff Peak above Ojai, this small camp with one stove, a table, and a hitching post has a dependable spring as a water supply. It suffered severe fire damage in 1985.

From the roadhead in Gridley Canyon follow the reworked beginning of the Gridley Tral (22W05) up to the Nordhoff Fire Road and bear right. Follow this fire road moderately uphill to the camp through chaparral. From camp, the Gridley Trail continues moderately, then steeply, uphill to the crest of the Topatopa Mountains in 2 miles.
TOPO: *Ojai*

HADDOCK (6,080′) (5.8) This is a fairly large camp with four stoves and tables in the popular Pine Mountain backcountry section of the Los Padres. It is set on a rather open flat near the headwaters of Agua Blanca Creek. Pronounced "haydock," the camp is accessible from three points. The shortest is given here. The others are detailed in Trip Suggestion #'s 40, 41, 43, and 44.

From the roadhead at Reyes Peak Campground, continue driving along the Pine Mountain Road to its end. Walk along the closed dirt road for 0.2 miles and bear left onto the signed Reyes Peak Trail

(23W04). This footpath, which I consider a pleasure to hike, descends moderately along a ridge across alternating brushy, barren, and pine-covered slopes. Steep in sections, it reaches the camp at the junction of the Beartrap and Piedra Blanca trails in 5.8 miles. There are scattered pines at camp and a seasonal water supply.

TOPOS: *San Guillermo, Reyes Peak*

HAPPY HOLLOW (4,286′)(6.5) Nestled in an upended gully on Little Pine Mountain and sheltered by tall Coulter pines and sturdy Kellogg oaks, this camp is aptly named. It is furnished with two wilderness stoves and four tables and is a frequent stopover for backpackeers entering the San Rafael Wilderness from the south. But visitors would no doubt be happier with a water supply. Be sure to pack along an adequate supply for this long hike up, over, and around Little Pine Mountain. If you brought your tent along, I'd advise that you pitch it as Happy Hollow tends to retain cool nighttime moisture and saturate everything with a layer of early morning dew.

From Upper Oso Roadhead, follow the Camuesa Fire Road (5N15) for 0.8 miles. Bear left at a sharp turn in the road onto the Santa Cruz Trail (27W09) and hike up Oso Canyon past some fine fishing and wading pools. You pass the spur trail to Nineteen Oaks Camp and then begin a moderate, sometimes steep ascent, switchbacking through chaparral, in and out of shallow canyons, with shade granted by an occasional bigcone spruce or ponderosa pine. At 4,300 feet, 5 miles from the roadhead, the trail reaches Alexander Saddle where a clear day will give you a gorgeous view far out to sea. Bear right here and walk up into Happy Hollow Camp. Water is available about a mile and a half west of the camp at Little Pine Spring.

TOPOS: *Little Pine Mountain, San Marcos Pass.* F/C

HAPPY HUNTING GROUNDS (3,500′)(10.5) Used early in this century as a base camp for hunting excursions into Hurricane Deck and into the wildest reaches of the Santa Barbara Backcountry, this small camp beneath a grand oak has two stoves. White Ledge Creek, a tributary of the South Fork of the Sisquoc River seasonally flows nearby. The camp is within the San Rafael Wilderness.

From NIRA Roadhead follow the instructions to Manzana Narrows

Camp. Continue upstream 0.4 miles to a junction. Your route stays left on the Manzana Trail (30W13) and climbs above the headwaters of Manzana Creek to a ridge, then descends to the wilderness camp, 3.5 miles beyond the Narrows.

TOPOS: *Hurricane Deck, San Rafael Mountain, Figueroa Mountain, Bald Mountain.* F/C, W/A

HEATH (3,440′)(17.8) One of the favorite fishing and hunting retreats of old Jim Heath, a local rancher and friend of Teddy Roosevelt, this San Rafael Wilderness camp is on a flat along the Sisquoc River at the mouth of Judell Canyon. With reliable swimming, drinking, and fishing water nearby, two stoves and ample shade, this might well become one of your favorite haunts too, especially in the springtime.

From Santa Barbara Canyon Roadhead follow the Big Pine Road (9N11) west for 3 miles to the Sierra Madre Road (32S19). Turn right and continue to the beginning of Judell Trail (26W05) on Santa Barbara Potrero. Turn south down Judell Trail. In 4.7 miles, you reach the bottom of Sisquoc Canyon and walk into Heath Camp.

TOPOS: *Big Pine Mountain, Salisbury Potrero, Fox Mountain.* F/C, W/A

HIDDEN POTRERO (2,700′)(3.0) Just off the Camuesa Fire Road (5N15), this camp with stoves, tables and a spring is only rarely visited by hikers. Weekends are noisy here with bikers.

From Upper Oso Roadhead, travel the well-graded Camuesa Road (5N15) uphill 3 miles to the camp.

TOPOS: *Little Pine Mountain, San Marcos Pines.*

INDIAN CAVE (2,970′)(7.1) Most Indian sites leave me with a feeling of sadness. I feel here more than anywhere else that our scientific, logical society has numbed our awareness of a sensitivity and intuitive understanding perceived by primitive people. I come to places like this to try to find what I know we've lost. At this site there is a cave with rock paintings. The adjacent canyon was used as a hunting ground and trading route between the Santa Clara and Cuyama valleys. There are no Forest Service facilities. Water is not to be counted on in summer.

From the roadhead at Dough Flat follow the instructions for Alder Creek Camp. At the junction below Dripping Springs, 5.6 miles from the start, bear right onto the Alder Creek Trail (20W11). Follow the streambed briefly, then climb up and over a low ridge to meet and cross Alder Creek. Travel upstream to another crossing and then to the camp, 1.5 miles from the junction. Only a fool would damage the priceless weathered pictographs here.

TOPO: *Devils Heart Peak*

KERRY (2,200′)(2.4) Kerry is located on an established motorcycle trail in the far northern corner of the southern Los Padres Forest. This small camp with a seasonal water supply and a single table and stove is visited mainly by hikers who prefer noise. The trail is in terrible shape.

From the roadhead at Pine Flat, hike down the moderately steep Kerry Canyon Trail (30W02). Follow the bike trail as best you can a total of 2.4 miles downstream to the camp.

TOPOS: *Branch Mountain, Manzanita Mountain*

LADY BUG (4,800′)(12.3) Appropriately named for the concentrations of lady bugs that, for some reason, occur in the area, this camp is located on the popular Red Reef Trail in Timber Canyon and features one stove. A nearby spring provides water when the creek runs dry. Although it's a strenuous hike to the camp, you'll enjoy dramatic views of the Topatopa Bluffs and Ridge, Hines Peak (6,704 feet), and the entire Ojai Valley.

From Sisar Canyon Roadhead follow the Sisar Canyon Fire Road (4N15) on a moderate 2.8-mile ascent. At the point where the road makes a hairpin turn, continue north onto the Red Reef Trail (21W08) and follow it a steep 2.8 miles to White Ledge Camp (Ventura County). Continue steeply up Sisar Canyon beyond the camp, enjoying views of attractive Topatopa Bluffs as you switchback up to a junction on the Topatopa Ridge in 1.8 miles. Turn right (east) onto the Topatopa Fire Road (5N08) and follow it along the ridge to another junction with an abandoned trail down Santa Paula Canyon. You stay left here, and follow the road a total of 3.4 miles to its end behind Hines Peak.

Bear north onto the Red Reef Trail and descent 1.5 miles to Lady Bug Camp.

TOPOS: *Santa Paula Peak, Ojai, Topatopa Mountains*

LITTLE MUTAU (5,250′)(3.8) Set in a rather dry canyon amid piñon pines and stream alders, this camp with a single stove is hospitable and enjoyable in spring when creek water can be relied upon.

From the roadhead at Mutau Flat, follow the Little Mutau Trail (20W10) due west on a moderate to steep ascent 2 miles to a saddle. Descend to Little Mutau Creek on a moderate grade and continue upstream to reach the camp in another 1.2 miles.

TOPOS: *McDonald Peak, Lockwood Valley*

LITTLE PINE SPRING (3,350′)(7.3) A small camp set in the shadow of Alexander Peak, Little Pine offers shade, views, and a single table and stove. Don't expect total seclusion, however, as the camp also has the only reliable water along this portion of the Santa Cruz Trail. Campers staying at nearby Happy Hollow Camp regularly use this spring to tank up.

From Oso Roadhead, follow the directions provided to Happy Hollow Camp as far as Alexander Saddle, 6 miles. From there, continue downhill through oaks and digger pines along the Santa Cruz Trail (27W09) for 1 mile. As the main trail begins to veer northeast, watch on the left for a well worn but signed path. Follow that path a steep quarter-mile down to the camp.

TOPOS: *Little Pine Mountain, San Marcos Pass.* F/C

LOG CABIN (1,510′)(4.5) This camp is located on a small flat next to the narrow defile of the Devil's Gateway and shaded by oaks. It has four stoves, one table, and a dependable water source in Agua Blanca Creek, the stream of "white water." Firearms are prohibited in the area. Poison oak is plentiful.

From the roadhead at Blue Point Campground, walk upstream and cross Piru Creek. Pass through the locked gate onto the Whitaker Ranch property and continue up the dirt road until it reaches Agua Blanca Creek. Turn left (west) and follow the creekbed until the Agua Blanca Trail (19W10) picks up at a register just past a cabin. Hike the Agua Blanca Trail all the way to the camp, a total of 5 miles from

the start. Where this unmaintained trail is washed out you must travel in streambed, but the upstream route is always obvious. When you reach the Devil's Gateway, you have the option of wading a short distance through a narrows or following a steep trail up and around the Gateway to the camp. Fishing might be worthwhile in season.
TOPO: *Cobblestone Mountain.* F/C

LONNIE DAVIS (2,640')(12.5) Alonzo Davis was the head of a pioneer family that settled in the Manzana Canyon in the late 19th century. He went on to become one of the first forest rangers in the Santa Barbara Backcountry. This San Rafael Wilderness camp bearing his name is located near the northern terminus of the Manzana Trail by a flat where the trail reaches the South Fork of the Sisquoc. Because of its location in the center of the wilderness near two trail junctions, Lonnie Davis makes a fine base camp for exploration of the heart of this 151,000-acre primitive area. Three stoves and a dependable water supply await you.

From NIRA Roadhead, follow the Manzana Trail (30W13) on a moderate but tiring 6.2-mile ascent to Manzana Camp. Continue 1.2 miles upstream, passing through Manzana Narrows, to a trail junction. Bear left here and, still on the Manzana Trail, ascend the hot and dusty footpath to the top of 4,160-foot Hurricane Deck. You hike down easily to Happy Hunting Grounds, 3.1 miles. It's another easy mile to pleasant White Ledge Camp, where you bear right at a junction with the Hurricane Trail to descend a sometimes steep switchbacking 2 miles to Lonnie Davis. The camp is located on the east bank of the South Fork of the Sisquoc, a quarter-mile before the South Fork Guard Station. The route to this camp is described in more detail in the "Great Circle Route," Trip #53.
TOPOS: *Hurricane Deck, Bald Mountain, San Rafael Mountain, Figueroa Mountain.* W/A

LOST VALLEY (1.925')(1.0) Just a short hike into the San Rafael Wilderness, this little camp is frequently passed but seldom used. It has one stove with water available from nearby Manzana Creek. Golden wildflowers near the camp add beautiful color in spring. The camp is shaded by oaks and digger pines.

From the NIRA Roadhead follow the Manzana Trail (30W13) upstream across the creek and on an easy 1-mile hike to the oak-shaded camp at the junction with the Lost Valley Trail (29W14) up to Hurricane Deck. From here, the Manzana Trail continues upcanyon to the creek's headwaters.

TOPO: *Bald Mountain.* W/A

LOWER ALAMAR (2,880′)(10.9) This camp with two stoves and two tables is set in remote Alamar Canyon below the summit of the Loma Pelona (4,452 feet). It was once used as a base camp for an official wildlife inventory of this area because of its central location. A telephone line installed by the U.S.F.S. actually extended to this remote location at one time. The water supply is seasonal from the adjacent creek.

From Mono Roadhead continue up to the locked gate at Little Caliente Hot Springs and start walking up the Mono-Alamar Trail (5N33), actually a jeep road. The going is easy as you continue past the Oglivy Ranch in 3.7 miles, where the road retires to a footpath (27W07) and travels through numerous stream crossings and washouts to Mono Narrows Camp, 6.8 miles from the start.

Three-quarters of a mile farther on, the Mono-Alamar Trail (26W16) leaves the canyon to climb steeply up the "Caracole" before dropping to a trail junction in 2 miles. Turn right (east) here and follow the Alamar Hill Trail down into Alamar Canyon to reach the camp in 1.5 additional miles.

TOPOS: *Little Pine Mountain, Madulce Peak, Hildreth Peak.* F/C, W/A

LOWER BEAR (5,080′)(14.4) Allegedly named for a pioneer who was snowed in at this spot and had to subsist on the meat from a bear he shot, this site is at the top of the notorious Devil's Slide on the Sisquoc Trail. Just downstream, Sisquoc Falls tumbles majestically down into the canyon. Because of its high subalpine setting near the headwaters of the Sisquoc, and its green grasses, tall trees and deep blue sky, I find this spot reminiscent of some of my favorite Sierra Nevada hideaways. Although it is a long and dusty hike to get here, this camp setting makes it perfect for the person or group desiring a peaceful and refreshing few days rest. You will find two stoves, one table, and a dependable water supply.

From Santa Barbara Canyon Roadhead follow the directions given above 13.7 miles to Bear Camp. From Bear, follow the Sisquoc Trail (27W07) 0.7 miles down to Lower Bear Camp.

TOPOS: *Big Pine Mountain, Salisbury Potrero, Fox Mountain, Madulce Peak.* F/C, W/A

LOWER BUCKHORN (1,960′)((6.6) Located on Buckhorn Creek, a tributary of Indian Canyon, near the site of a legendary Chumash hunting camp, Lower Buckhorn offers two stoves, a table, and a seasonal water supply.

From Mono Roadhead, follow the Camuesa Fireroad (5N15) through two stream crossings to the start of the Indian Creek Trail marked by a locked gate across an old jeep road on the right. Turn onto this old road and hike through two creek crossings and over a small hill for 0.9 miles to a point where you see the unsigned Indian Creek Trail (27W12) take off on the left. Follow this twisty, windy pathway 3.2 miles to a junction with the Buckhorn Trail (27W12). Bear left here and follow the trail a short ways up Buckhorn Canyon to the camp.

TOPO: *Little Pine Mountain.* F/C

MADULCE (5,000′)(6.0) Named for its proximity to the nearby peak, Madulce (which means "strawberry" in Catalonian Spanish) refers to the tasty wild fruits that grow in this portion of the Santa Barbara Backcountry. The camp is located near the headwaters of Pine Creek, is attractively forested with pine, fir, cedar, and oak, and has five well-spaced stoves and a single table. Stream water is reliable except in the driest of years and there is also a spring below camp. Nearby is the historic Madulce Guard Station built by the Forest Service in 1930. It was recently restored and is now listed on the National Register of Historic Places. For the story of this station, see Trip #50.

From Santa Barbara Canyon Roadhead walk due south on the Santa Barbara Canyon Trail (25W02), really a retiring jeep road, which easily gains altitude as it follows the creek upstream. Five miles in, as you near the stream's headwaters, the trail heads south up a tributary

canyon, climbs more steeply to cross over a ridge, and descends in a mile to the camp and cabin on Pine Creek.
TOPOS: *Madulce Peak, Fox Mountain.* F/C, W/A

MANSFIELD (3,000 ') (16.3) Also known as Sisquoc Falls Camp, this stopover is only a short hike away from the beautiful waterfalls on Rattlesnake Creek. Since it is also just upstream from the Sisquoc Condor Sanctuary, your chance for seeing one of the rare birds is improved. The camp has six separate sites spread over a large flat. There are good fishing and swimming holes in the Sisquoc River.

From NIRA Roadhead follow the instructions given above 12.5 miles to Lonnie Davis Camp. From there, continue 0.8 miles to South Fork Camp. Turn east onto Sisquoc Trail (27W07) and hike an easy 2 miles to Skunk Camp and 1 more mile to Mansfield.
TOPOS: *Hurricane Deck, Bald Mountain, San Rafael Mountain, Figueroa Mountain, Big Pine Mountain, Salisbury Potrero.* W/A

MANZANA (2,000') (6.2) A refreshing half-day hike into the San Rafael Wilderness along the Manzana Trail will take the willing hiker to this canyon camp with two stoves, dependable water, fishing and swimming pools. Sturdy live oaks and colorful manzanita shade the spot.

From the NIRA Roadhead follow the Manzana Trail (30W13) across Manzana Creek and southeast into the wilderness. The route crosses a low ridge where digger pines grow and arrives at Lost Valley Camp and a junction with the Lost Valley Trail (29W14) to Hurricane Deck in 1 mile. Continuing upstream along the Manzana, you travel above the wide streambed past Fish Creek Camp to another stream crossing in 3.4 miles. You remain close to the edge of the streambed most of the remaining 1.8 miles and walk into Manzana Camp just after crossing a reliable tributary creek. Portions of this trip abound with wildflowers in spring. In 1983 I counted over two dozen different species along the Manzana Trail.
TOPOS: *San Rafael Mountain, Figueroa Mountain, Bald Mountain.* W/A

MANZANA NARROWS (2,960′)(7.0) Lodged in the narrows of Manzana Creek where there are pools for wading or fishing, this camp has four stoves and a single table. Water is plentiful with the largest swimming hole along the Manzana just downstream. For a day of sitting around, listening to gurgling water and blowing wind, come here.

From the NIRA Roadhead follow the directions just given 6.2 miles to Manzana Camp. Continue upstream on the Manzana Trail (30W13) for 0.8 miles to this oak- and willow-shaded camp.
TOPOS: San Rafael Mountain, Figueroa Mountain, Bald Mountain.
W/A

MANZANA SCHOOLHOUSE (1,000′) (7.8) Easily the largest, lowest, and most popular backcountry campsite in this part of the Los Padres National Forest, this camp is located on a roomy, grassy, oak-shaded flat at the confluence of Manzana Creek and the Sisquoc River. With eight widely spaced stoves and six tables, there is room for several camping groups. I suggest avoiding this popular spot on Easter weekend. There is also the historic schoolhouse, another interesting remnant of Hiram Wheat's late 19th-century settlement in the Sisquoc and Manzana canyons. (See Trip #55.)

From the NIRA Roadhead cross Manzana Creek on the Sunset Valley Road and bear right onto the Manzana Trail (30W13) heading northeast and downstream. You travel on a well-constructed footpath high above the stream for nearly 1 mile and then descend a set of switchbacks, cross the stream, and enter Potrero Camp at a junction with the Indian Caves Trail. You remain on the Manzana Trail 1.8 more easy miles to Coldwater Camp and then continue for 5 additional miles to Manzana Schoolhouse. There are nearly a dozen stream crossings during this hike and so the route is not recommended for travel during or immediately after stormy weather. During the last 5 miles, the trail travels away from Manzana Creek a number of times, passing through some of the most beautiful meadows in Southern California. These grasslands are ablaze with wildflowers in the spring.
TOPOS: *Zaca Lake, Bald Mountain.*W/A

MAPLE (3,800′)(0.6) Located on the slope of Ortega Hill in an area where bigleaf maple, western chokecherry, and bigcone spruce grow, this camp is an easy dayhike or overnight backpack. There are two stoves and a regular water supply here from a tributary of Matilija Creek.

From the roadhead near Cherry Creek Campground, follow the Ortega Hill Fire Road (6N01) ot the top of the Ortega Divide. If you're feeling adventurous, the remaining 650 feet to the summit of Ortega Hill are easily climbed. I suggest the ascent for its fine views in all directions, which help to put the area into perspective. From the divide, travel downhill on the Matilija Trail (23W07) 0.6 miles to Maple Camp. You can also reach Maple via a longer, steeper hike up Matilija Canyon from the Matilija Roadhead. There was fire damage to this area in 1985.

TOPO: *Wheeler Springs.* F/C

MATILIJA (1,740 ')(1.0) Its location on the shady north fork of Matilija Creek a mere half hour's hike from the roadhead makes this a perfect destination for an afternoon picnic. There are five stoves here and a table, so bring the hamburgers along. You might also want to bring some wood as the area is short on fuel, but water is plentiful from the creek. Unfortunately Matilija Camp and the access trail suffered damage during the fires and floods of 1985–86. Forest Service plans, however, call for complete repairs.

From the Matilija Roadhead hike on the level along the chaparral-lined Murietta Fire Road (5N13) for 0.4 miles to a crossing of Matilija Creek. Instead of crossing, bear right and walk up the first canyon to the right (north). Continue crosscountry to the camp in 0.6 miles. Stream erosion here has created dramatic evidence on the canyon wall of uplifts along the Santa Ynez Fault.

TOPO: *Old Man Mountain.* F/C

MATTIAS POTRERO (1,600 ')(1.3) This fairly new trail camp is set on a small meadow on the northern slopes of the Santa Ynez Mountains. Two stoves and a table are provided and water is seasonal from a nearby creek.

From the roadhead near Santa Ynez Campground follow the Mattias Potrero Trail (27W25) steeply south up the chaparral-covered mountain for 1.1 miles. Bear left at a junction and travel easily east-southeast on Trail 27W19 the remaining 0.2 miles to the camp. **TOPO:** *Little Pine Mountain.*

McDONALD (4,150′)(7.7) Located at the ruins of a miner's old stone cabin, this camp on seasonal Alder Creek is shaded by bigcone spruce, laurel, and oak. It has two stoves.

From the roadhead at Mutau Flat follow the Little Mutau Trail (20W10) east. You climb, steeply at times, 2 miles to a saddle, then descend 1.8 miles to the floor of Little Mutau Canyon where there is a campsite. You follow the canyon downstream and then begin climbing moderately up another saddle, reached in 1.8 miles. Bearing right (20W11) at a junction, you finally descend a steep switchbacking 2.1 miles to McDonald Camp on Alder Creek. **TOPOS:** *McDonald Peak, Lockwood Valley*

McGUIRE (5,300′)(1.3) High on the north slope of Pine Mountain, this small camp offers spectacular views of the rugged Cuyama Badlands in the Mt. Piños Country. Despite the popularity of the area, McGuire seems little used and makes a fine destination for a dayhike or overnighter. You will find two wilderness stoves and a reliable spring here. And, if you can arrange to leave a second car, you can turn this into a downhill shuttle trip by continuing on the well-maintained Ozena Trail down to the ranger station below.

From Pine Mountain Roadhead, hike onto the Ozena Trail (23W03) and head off north through the pines. You soon begin descending along a tributary of Boulder Canyon. After 1 mile, watch to the west for a side trail which descends an easy quarter-mile to the camp. **TOPO:** *Reyes Peak*

McKINLEY SPRING (5,600′)(10.0) A little-known trail camp not shown on most maps, this site is located on the northern chaparral-covered slope of McKinley Mountain. It offers two stoves, nearby water (except in summer) from a spring, and some all-encompassing views of the San Rafael Wilderness.

From the roadhead at Cachuma Saddle, follow steep and winding Fire Road 8N08 east as it curls around the summit of Cachuma Mountain. Continue on the road on a slight descent to reach Hell's Half Acre in 5.2 miles. The road ascends through a small forested area, then descends above the headwaters of Manzana Creek. It finally rises again to reach exposed McKinley Spring Camp in 4.8 miles. I suggest climbing the 6,182-foot peak nearby to experience Santa Barbara County at your feet.

TOPOS: *San Rafael Mountain, Figueroa Mountain.* F/C

MESA SPRING (6,000′)(3.5) Almost unknown and seldom-visited, this small camp is southwest of the summit of Cerro Noroeste (Mt. Abel) and is reasily reachable only by a round-about route. It has three stoves. Water is from the tank at Mesa Spring in camp.

From the roadhead on Cerro Noroeste follow Trail 21W03 southwest and downhill toward Mt. Piños. In 0.7 miles a junction is reached. Bear right onto Trail 22W01 and steeply descend along a small tributary. As the trail begins to level off, it leaves the streambed and travels to reach Mesa Spring Camp in 2.8 miles.

TOPO: *Sawmill Mountain.*

MIDDLE CALIENTE (2,150′)(1.0) Recently restored to a useable condition through the generous efforts of the Lompoc Search and Rescue Team, this campsite with three tables and a wilderness stove makes a fine picnic destination before or after enjoying the hot springs at Big Caliente.

From Big Caliente Roadhead follow the Agua Caliente Trail (25W06) north past a debris dam and past the mouth of Diablo Canyon. Continue hiking streamside through the chaparral to the camp. There is a large pool a short way below camp, but stream water cannot always be counted upon in summer.

TOPO: *Hildreth Peak.* F/C

MIDDLE CAMUESA (1,920 ')(7.0) Located on the Camuesa Road Motorcycle Way, this camp is usually avoided by hikers. It has two stoves and a seasonal water supply.

From the roadhead at Mono Campground follow the Camuesa Fire Road (5N15) to the locked gate. Continue on the road moderately uphill through chaparral for 7 miles to the camp.

TOPO: *Little Pine Mountain.* F/C

MIDDLE MATILIJA (2,380 ')(3.1). Even through damaged during the fires and floods of 1985–1986, this camp on the north fork of the Matilija Creek is still a pleasant stopover. It has two stoves and is shaded by live oaks. It is an easy half-day hike from the trailhead, just far enough away from civilization to make for a refreshing overnight backpack trip.

Fire Road (5N13) for 0.4 miles to a crossing of Matilija Creek. Instead of crossing here, bear right and hike up the first canyon to the right (north). Continue 0.6 miles crosscountry to Matilija Camp. From here, travel upstream for 2.5 miles on a moderate to easy ascent along a jeep road that is washed out in sections. A little ways before you reach the camp the road narrows into the Matilija Trail (23W07). The trail continues out of the camp and travels to Maple Camp below Ortega Hill.

TOPOS: *Wheeler Springs, Old Man Mountain.* F/C

MILLER CANYON (1600 ')(16.8) Another remote San Rafael Wilderness camp on the Sisquoc River, Miller is near ruins of the Miller homestead of the late 19th century. Fishing and swimming holes are nearby, and the water supply is always reliable. Facilities include two stoves and a table. The camp is usually used by parties with stock and so is not especially desirable for backpackers.

From the NIRA Roadhead follow the detailed directions provided for the 7.8-mile trek to Manzana Schoolhouse Camp. Then turn northeast onto the Sisquoc Trail (30W12) and hike upcanyon 9 miles through through several stream crossings past Water Canyon and Mormon camps to Miller, on the Sisquoc at the foot of Miller Canyon. Miller is 2.5 miles upstream from Mormon Camp.

TOPOS: *Bald Mountain, Zaca Lake.* W/A

MINE CAMP (3,800′)(2.0) Located in Bear Canyon near the edge of the Dick Smith Wilderness, this camp, virtually ignored by the public, makes for an attractive picnic destination in spring. Shade provided by pine and spruce coupled with a northern exposure keeps the canyon cool, and you'll find two tables, two stoves, and ample firewood here. There is no water in or near camp.

From Bear Roadhead on CAL 33, walk past the locked gate and onto the retiring jeep road known as the Deal Trail (24W04). The trail climbs easily then a tad more moderately up Bear Canyon to reach the camp in 2 miles. For a loop trip to this site, see Trip #45.
TOPOS: *Reyes Peak, Rancho Nuevo Creek.*

MISSION PINE BASIN (5,400′)(21.1) One of the most secluded camps in the San Rafael Wilderness, this small retreat has two stoves and one table, but no convenient water supply. Located in a beautiful grove of coulter pine, it was originally established in 1924 as a trail maintenance camp.

From the roadhead at Upper Oso Campground follow the directions provided above for 17.3 miles to Coche Camp via Santa Cruz Camp. At Coche fill your canteens and follow the steep, switchbacking Santa Cruz Trail (27W09) through dense chaparral on a hot and tiring hike 3.8 tough miles to the shady basin camp. Mission Pine Basin normally receives snow in winter. In a pinch, water can usually be found down in the watershed of Fall Creek.
TOPOS: *Big Pine Mountain, San Rafael Mountain, San Marcos Pass, Little Pine Mountain.* F/C, W/A

MISSION PINE SPRING 5,840′)(27.7) Legend has it that Jeffrey and sugar pines were logged from the forested slopes of San Rafael Mountain in the days of the padres to provide sturdy wood beams for the construction of the famous Santa Barbara Mission. Whether the story is apocryphal or not, this conifer-covered flat makes for fine camping during the cooler months of the year. It is remote, secluded, and truly beautiful. There is snow here in winter. At the site are two stoves and tables. This camp has the one thing Mission Pine Basin (above) lacks: a reliable spring.

From Upper Oso Roadhead follow the directions just given 21.1 miles to Mission Pine Basin. There, turn due west onto the Mission Pine Trail (28W01) and trek across the chaparral-covered crest of the San Rafael Mountains for 3.3. miles gently uphill to the pine-shaded camp. There are expansive views of the surrounding countryside to be enjoyed on the hike along the ridge trail. The summit of San Rafael Mountain (6,593 feet) is easily climbed by continuing another 2.2 miles west along the Mission Pine Trail.

TOPOS: *San Rafael Mountain, Big Pine Mountain, Little Pine Mountain, San Marcos Pass.* F/C, W/A

MONO NARROWS (2,100′)(6.8) Since its location does not appear on many maps, Mono Narrows is often overlooked. Although it has only a single stove, the camp offers swimming pools and nearby waterfalls. The narrows of Mono Creek upstream can be a delight to explore.

From Mono Roadhead drive up Fire Road 5N33 to the locked gate at Little Caliente Hot Springs. Hike north beyond here on the jeep trail that's part of the Mono-Almar Trail. The road changes its number to 6N30 then to 26W07 as it continues past the private Ogilvy Ranch reached in 3.7 miles. A bit more ruggedly now, a footpath continues up Mono Creek another 3.1 miles to the camp just below the Narrows.

TOPOS: *Hildreth Peak, Little Pine Mountain.* F/C

MORMON (1,400′)(14.3) With two stoves, this wilderness camp on the Sisquoc River is near the gravesite of a member of the Hiram Wheat settlement. Contrary to popular belief, this religious group was not Mormon but followed similar religious precepts.

From NIRA Roadhead follow the Manzana Trail (30W13) 7.8 miles northwest according to the directions I've provided to Manzana Schoolhouse Camp. Turn northwest onto the Sisquoc Canyon Trail (30W12) and hike this sandy route upriver through streambed and across grassy meadowland. As you approach Water Canyon Camp in 4.3 miles, you'll begin to notice the ruins left by the turn-of-the-century homesteaders. Another 2.2 miles will take you into oak-shaded Mormon Camp near the foot of Wellman Canyon.

TOPOS: *Bald Mountain, Zaca Lake.* W/A

MURIETTA (1,810 ′)(1.0) One of my favorite springtime haunts is this little camp on reliable Murietta Creek. At that time of the year the underbrush is green, the creek is at full flow, and tasty miner's lettuce can be found along the trail. I highly recommend it for a picnic or overnight campout. The site features four stoves and three tables on a shaded flat. There was some fire damage in 1985.

From Matilija Roadhead, hike upstream along the dirt road (24W07), soon crossing Matilija Creek. Continue on the road a short distance to an unmarked junction on the left. Turn left onto a dirt road here and hike up Murietta Canyon. The road soon narrows into a trail that crosses the creek twice before arriving at this little camp on a streamside flat. Shade is provided by cedar, live oak, and toyon.

TOPOS: *White Ledge Peak, Old Man Mountain.* F/C

NINETEEN OAKS (1,680 ′)(1.9) Set on a small, oak-shaded knoll near a spring of questionable quality, this camp is an all right destination for a picnic or overnighter. There are three stoves here with drinking water available from nearby Oso Creek (purify!).

From Upper Oso Roadhead continue past the locked gate and on up the Camuesa Fire Road (5N15), a motorcycle route, for 0.8 miles. Bear left at the junction with the Santa Cruz Trail (27W09) and follow it along Oso Creek for 1 mile to a junction with a spur to the right. Follow the spur trail up to the camp.

TOPO: *San Marcos Pass.*

OAK (4,500 ′)(2.0) I am fond of little Oak Camp. Lodged beneath several low, spreading live oaks on the bank of the Chorro Grande, it is practically hidden from view. It offers three stoves, seasonal water, and quiet repose.

From Chorro Grande Roadhead follow the Chorro Grande Trail (23W05) easily uphill. After a short way the trail briefly joins a dirt road (stay left) and then continues up the small, peaceful, chaparral-lined canyon to the camp, marked by a sign, on the left. From here the Chorro Grande Trail continues steeply uphill to Chorro Grande Springs.

TOPO: *Wheeler Springs*

PAINTED ROCK (4,600 ')(7.0) Painted Rock was used as a Chumash Indian hunting and gathering encampment centuries ago. The location is ideal. Nearby Montgomery Potrero supports five reliable springs with ample forage to attract wildlife. The high meadow is colored golden with deep blue hues in the springtime. A series of shallow sandstone caves decorated with baffling pictographs speak of a time when life was simpler and more meaningful, when shamans and medicine men would watch the condors soaring high over Hurricane Deck and speak intimately with the gods. The Forest Service provides three stoves and a table here.

From McPherson Roadhead follow the Sierra Madre Fire Road (32S13) southeast for an up and down 7 miles to the camp. The hike is long but easy. From Painted Rock, the Jackson Trail (27W06) travels down into the Sisquoc Canyon. The Sierra Madre Road continues to Salisbury Potrero and beyond. For another route to Painted Rock, see Trip #54.

TOPOS: *Hurricane Deck, Peak Mountain.*

PELCH (3,775 ')(20.5) Located at the southwestern edge of the San Rafael Wilderness, Pelch is one of the less frequently visited camps in this area because of the long dry route along the Big Pine Fire Road (open to motorcycles) required to reach it. At Pelch there are three campsites and a reliable source of water from the east fork of Grapevine Creek. For a longer alternative route to Pelch through the wilderness, see Trip #51.

From the roadhead at Upper Oso Campground, follow the Camuesa Fire Road (5N15) past Hidden Potrero to a junction in 4 uphill miles. Bear left onto the Big Pine Road (6N13) and continue ascending 5 miles. Bear left onto the Big Pine Road (6N13) and continue ascending 5 miles to another junction near Little Pine Mountain. Bear right onto the Big Pine Fire Road (9N11) and continue another winding 10.5 miles to Bluff Camp and Field Station. Turn left here onto the Grapevine Trail (27W10) and follow it an easy 3 miles down to Pelch Camp.

TOPOS: *Big Pine Mountain, Little Pine Mountain, San Marco Pass.*
F/C, W/A

PENS (3,340′)(12.4) Sometimes called "Lower Poplar" and not appearing on many maps, this camp was named by early ranchers who built stockpens nearby. Traces of those pens are long gone, but this little camp deep in Indian Canyon is remote and pleasant in the cool months. Stream water is generally reliable. You'll find two stoves.

From the Mono Roadhead, drive up to the locked gate at Little Caliente Hot Springs and start walking up Fire Road 5N33. The going is easy as you follow the Mono-Alamar Trail on a jeep road (6N30) past the Ogilvy Ranch in 3.7 miles. It's a bit more difficult on the trail (27W07) to Mono Narrows, another 3.1 miles and a good overnight stop.

Three-quarters of a mile later the trail (26W16) leaves the canyon to climb steeply up "The Caracole" before dropping to a trail junction in two miles. Turn left (west) here and follow the Alamar Hill Trail up and over the "Loma Pelone" (Bald Head) and then down a tributary to the camp on Indian Creek. This camp has been mislabeled "Indian Can" on some recent maps.

TOPOS: *Little Pine Mountain, Big Pine Mountain, Hildreth Peak, Madulce Peak.* F/C, W/A

PIEDRA BLANCA (3,550′)(2.1) Dubbed "white rock" for the dominant sandstone formations in this part of the Sespe country, this camp offers four stoves, three tables and a reliable water source. It is a delightful place to spend a night any time of the year.

From Lion Roadhead, cross Sespe Creek on the Old Sespe Road and bear left almost immediately onto the Piedra Blanca Trail (22W03). As you climb easily through chaparral, you will pass the eroded sandstone formations — the "white rocks" that give "Piedra Blanca" its name. After 0.7 miles, the trail descends steeply by quick switchbacks into Piedra Blanca Canyon. You cross a tributary stream, then bear left up the main canyon. You continue hiking up along the attractive cascading creek all the way to the camp. Numerous old live oaks make the streamside site a shady place. The four campsites are separated by enough foliage to allow for privacy.

TOPO: *Lion Canyon*

PINE MOUNTAIN LODGE (6,000′)(5.3) This camp, with four wilderness stoves and a hitching post, is located at the site of a cabin that was built in the 1930s by a group of local hunters on the slope of Pine Mountain. Unfortunately, in an effort to remove an old oak tree that was leaning precariously toward the structure, a rope slipped, the tree fell and the cabin was crushed. All that remains today is its fireplace. The high elevation of this particular campsite makes it a green, cool overnight stop from February through June. There is a seasonal spring at camp. Snow visits in winter.

From Lion Roadhead, follow the Piedra Blanca Trail 2.4 miles according to the directions provided to Piedra Blanca Camp. From there, continue on the Piedra Blanca Trail (22W03) past Twin Forks Camp and climb moderately up the north fork of Piedra Blanca Creek for a mile and a half. Near the 4,800-foot level, the trail leaves the creek and climbs steeply toward the summit of Pine Mountain. At 6,000 feet, you top a rise where there is a junction with the spur trail to Piru Creek. Bear left here and continue an easy quarter-mile to Pine Mountain Lodge.

TOPO: *Lion Canyon*

POPLAR (3,360′)(12.9) Shaded by live oaks and cottonwoods in a chapparal-shrouded canyon, Poplar is remote and beautiful. Activities include exploring Indian Creek downstream or day hiking up to the Buckhorn Road for a view into the San Rafael Wilderness. The camp itself is within the bourndary of the Dick Smith Wilderness and has three stoves and an old table.

From the Mono Roadhead follow the directions given above to Pens Camp. Continue upstream on Trail 26W08 an easy half-mile to Poplar.

TOPOS: *Little Pine Mountain, Big Pine Mountain, Hildreth Peak, Madulce Peak.* F/C, W/A

POTRERO (1,750′)(1.0) This little trail camp is located at the junction of the Manzana and Indian Caves trails, an easy mile's hike into the San Rafael Wilderness. If you have a friend you'd like to introduce to backcountry camping this coming spring and don't want to tire him out on his first hike, this site is a good destination. Water is readily available from Manzana Creek.

From NIRA Roadhead follow the Sunset Valley Road back across the creek and bear right onto the Manzana Trail (30W13). Heading northeast, follow the well-constructed footpath downstream traveling

high above the creek. After almost a mile you descend by switchbacks, cross the stream, and reach Potrero Camp.
TOPO: *Bald Mountain.* W/A

POTRERO JOHN (4,400′)(1.6) Situated in a chaparral-covered canyon, this camp has four stoves, tables, and a seasonal water supply. It is set on an oak-shaded flat at the end of a trail that meanders through stream, woodland, and brush.

From Sespe Gorge Roadhead follow the well-maintained foot trail (22W06) up Potrero John Creek. The route starts out a bit steeply, but soon levels off as it climbs upcanyon. California quail seem to find the abundant chaparral in this canyon a pleasant haunt, and you should not be too surprised if you spook a covey out from the woodland growth as you walk along.

The trail meanders along the canyon floor for 1.5 miles before crossing a rough wooden bridge over the creek. It then enters Potrero John Camp, set on a flat shaded by live oaks. The trail ends just beyond camp.
TOPO: *Wheeler Springs*

POTRERO SECO (4,850′)(4.5) Spanish for "dry meadow," this camp is an easy hike from Highway 33. It contains two stoves but streamwater is unreliable. Nearby La Jolla Spring, however, usually runs all year.

From the roadhead at Pine Mountain Summit, hike past the locked gate on the west side of the highway and follow Fire Road 6N03 4.5 miles to the oak-shaded camp on an intermittent stream. Be sure to bear right at the two "Y's" in the road.
TOPO: *Rancho Nuevo Creek*

RASPBERRY SPRING (6,750′)(0.4) Unreachable because of deep snows in winter and muddy roads in springtime, Raspberry Spring Camp on Pine Mountain makes for a perfect, convenient retreat any other time of the year. Named for the wild berry plants that grow near the spring, the camp offers far-ranging vistas of the Cuyama Badlands to the north. The snowcapped peaks of the southern Sierra Nevada can also be seen on clear days. There are three stoves here.

From roadhead at Reyes Peak Campground find the first campsite at the northwest end of the campground and pick up the unmarked Raspberry Spring Trail. Follow it 0.4 miles north down a draw through ponderosa pine and white fir to the camp.

TOPO: *Reyes Peak*

ROQUE (2,920′)(2.0) Hidden in secluded Roque Canyon in the Sierra Madre Mountains on a seasonal stream, this site has three stoves. The sourrounding area is covered by thick chaparral. The trail, completely brushed over, is very difficult to follow.

From Roque Roadhead follow the Roque Canyon Trail (30W03) on a sometimes switchbacking 2-mile descent along the backbone of a steep ridge to the camp in a small forested hollow. The trail used to continue down canyon but has been largely washed out and is no longer maintained.

TOPOS: *Manzanita Mountain, Bates Canyon*

SADDLE SKIRT (3,050′)(7.1) Set at the edge of a small meadow near oaks, sycamores, and cottonwoods, this remote, seldom-visited camp at the foot of Cobblestone Mountain has two stoves and the pleasant surroundings of stream woodland. Water is generally reliable.

From Dough Flat Roadhead follow the directions given above to Ant Camp, a moderate 6.1-mile hike. From there, continue on the Agua Blanca Trail (19W10) upstream and across the creek. Climb the grassy knoll where lupine bloom in spring and hike up the canyon through several stream crossings to reach Saddle Skirt in 1 mile. The trail beyond the camp climbs several miles around Cobblestone Mountain, but it is in very poor shape and is not recommended for travel.

TOPO: *Devils Heart Peak.* F/C.

SANTA CRUZ (1,920′)(11.5) Set along a deep, reliable creek at the edge of the San Rafael Wilderness, this beautiful shady camp provides fishing, swimming, five stoves and tables, a U.S.F.S. Field Station, and a corral. Here also are the ruins of the Alexander Cabin, used as a base camp during cattle drives in the early 1900s. Santa Cruz is the gateway to the appealing backcountry of the southern San Rafael Wilderness.

From Upper Oso Roadhead follow the Camuesa Fire Road (5N15) for 0.8 miles. Bear left at a sharp bend in the road onto the Santa Cruz Trail (27W09) and hike up Oso Canyon past some fine fishing and wading pools. In 1 mile you pass the spur trail to Nineteen Oaks Camp and begin a moderate, sometimes steep ascent, switchbacking 3.2 miles through chaparral with some shade provided by an occasional bigcone spruce or ponderosa pine. At 4,300 feet, the trail reaches a saddle from which there are great views out to the Pacific Ocean. From the saddle you descend 1 mile to Little Pine Springs junction and continue downhill 5.5 additional miles where, by way of ridgetop and canyon, you reach Santa Cruz Camp.

TOPOS: *San Rafael Mountain, San Marcos Pass, Little Pine Mountain.* F/C

SESPE HOT SPRINGS (2,450′)(6.0) Bubbling from a scorched earthen fissure, Sespe Hot Springs provides the hottest natural mineral water in Southern California. Temperatures exceeding 210 degrees Fahrenheit are not uncommon. The all-year spring keeps a dozen or so downstream pools warm enough for comfortable bathing, and there is even a homemade sauna built just below the springs themselves. Although Sespe might sound like a perfect wilderness retreat, it has a number of disadvantages. You might think that the ideal time to visit the area is during the winter and early spring months. But while the hiking is cooler this time of year, Hot Springs Canyon is in the shade most of the day, causing the air to stay quite chilly. During the summer months, the area gets ungodly hot, with temperatures frequently exceeding 90 degrees. The exposed Johnson Ridge Trail, the easiest route to the Sespe Hot Springs, has long been open to motorcycle traffic. That means your hike down into the canyon and your stay there are going to be noisy, dusty, and generally unpleasant. Further, the area around the springs is rocky and devoid of vegetation, resembling, in the words of one hiker, "the landscape of the moon."

Yet, despite these shortcomings, a trip to the Sespe Hot Springs is worthwhile. The area is distinctly different from the rest of the Santa Barbara Backcountry, and should you tire of the company of the bikers, you can adjourn a short distance away to the quiet sandy shores and swimming holes of nearby Sespe Creek.

From Mutau Flat Roadhead follow Trail 20W10 a short distance southeast to its junction with the Johnson Ridge Trail (20W12). Bear right and follow this pathway south around large dry Mutau Flat. After leaving Mutau, your route descends moderately and sometimes steeply downhill for 5 miles along the backbone of Johnson Ridge via motorcycle trail all the way to the Old Sespe Road (7N03). There is no shade at all during the descent and an early start is well advised. At the Sespe Road, turn left and continue 0.3 miles up to Sespe Trail Camp. For other routes to the Hot Springs, see Trips #35 and #36.

TOPO: *Topatopa Mountains*

SEVEN PINES (5,000′)(3.2) Located on the Snowy Creek Motorcycle Trail, this camp, with three stoves and two tables, is used mostly by weekend bikers. The hike down this forested canyon to the pine- and cedar-shaded camp is scenic and restful if the throbbing intrusion of the machines can be tolerated. Best try this one on a weekday.

From the roadhead on Alamo Mountain, follow the Snowy Creek Trail (19W04) moderately downhill 3.1 miles to Snowy Creek and a trail junction. Turn right (south) onto the Big Cedar Trail (19W05) and hike 0.5 miles to Seven Pines Camp where water is available from the seasonal stream. The trail leading south from the camp connects with the abandoned Cobblestone Trail. The Snowy Creek Trail (19W04) continues northeast to join a dirt road at Piru Creek in 5.8 miles.

TOPO: *McDonald Peak*

SHADY (2,400′)(7.2) This little camp with a single stove deserves its name. It is nestled just above a narrows of Alder Creek under a gigantic live oak. Water is seasonal from the stream. If you desire a few days of quiet solitude, it is unlikely anyone will bother you here.

From Dough Flat follow the directions given above to Alder Creek Camp (6.2 miles). Continue downstream along the Alder Creek Trail (20W13) through riparian woodland for 0.8 miles to an unmarked but obvious junction. The spur on the left travels an easy 0.2 miles to Shady. If you find yourself climbing up and out of the canyon, you have missed the junction and gone a quarter-mile too far.

TOPO: *Devils Heart Peak*

SHEEP (8,200′)(2.5) Used as a base camp by San Joaquin Valley ranchers in the early 1900s, this is one of the highest trail camps in the Los Padres National Forest. It is located in a shallow mountain valley on the southern timbered slope of Sawmill Mountain. Often covered by deep snows in winter, it is the terminus of the Mount Piños Skiway, a crosscountry ski route, which begins at the Chula Vista parking lot on Mt. Piños and travels 5.5 miles by snow-covered dirt road and trail to the camp. When the snows melt, the dirt road can be driven the 3 miles to the roadhead at the Condor Observation Point. The camp has four stoves and a spring. Water should be purified.

From the roadhead on Mt. Piños, follow Trail 21W07 as it descends an open slope via switchbacks, crosses a saddle, and begins ascending the pine-covered slopes of Sawmill Mountain on a moderate grade. After passing close by the Sawmill summit, the trail gently descends to a junction in 2 miles. Turn left (south) and hike down through Indian paintbrush and wild iris on the North Fork Trail (22W02) to reach the camp in another 0.5 miles. The trail out of camp descends to Lilly Meadows Camp and the Three Falls Boy Scout Facility. From the above-mentioned junction, Trail 21W03 climbs to the top of Cerro Noroeste (Mt. Abel) in 2.7 miles.

TOPO: *Sawmill Mountain*

SKUNK (2,800′)(16.3) No doubt named to commemorate some back-country traveler's unpleasant experience, this wilderness camp with two stoves has the unique attribute of being located directly across the Sisquoc River from the Condor Sanctuary. It is a small but pleasant spot set on a flat above the river. The water supply is dependable.

From the NIRA Roadhead follow the directions given below to the South Fork Camp (14.3 miles). Then continue upstream on the Sisquoc Trail (27W07), climbing moderately, then easily, the 2 miles to Skunk.

TOPOS: *Big Pine Mountain, Salisbury Potrero, Hurricane Deck, Peak Mountain.* F/C, W/A

SLUICE BOX (1,600′)(11.8) Although the site of past mining operations, this camp with two stoves and a table was probably named for the sluice-like channel eroded here by Horse Canyon Creek. The surrounding area is thick with chaparral. Water is seasonal in Horse Canyon.

From the NIRA Roadhead follow the detailed directions provided for 7.8 miles to Manzana Schoolhouse Camp. There, turn west and travel down the Sisquoc Trail (30W12), actually an old wagon road, 1.8 miles to a junction on the right with the Horse Gulch Trail (31W09). Follow this brushy trail easily up Horse Canyon through several stream crossings to reach the camp in 2.2 miles.

TOPOS: *Bald Mountain, Zaca Lake*

SOUTH FORK (2,520′)(14.3) South Fork might well be called the "crossroads of the San Rafael Wilderness" since the primitive area's two major trails, the Sisquoc and Manzana, meet at this campsite deep in the Santa Barbara Backcountry. You will find ample water for swimming, fishing, and drinking here at the confluence of the Sisquoc River with its reliable South Fork. The camp itself is roomy and is provided with five stoves. If you're looking for a centrally located basecamp at which to hang out for a few days while you explore the San Rafael, this spot is perfect.

From NIRA Roadhead, follow the detailed directions I've provided to either Manzana or Manzana Narrows camps for your first day's hike. From there, continue along the Manzana Trail (30W13) a short way to a junction. Bear left here and switchback up and over Hurricane Deck 3.5 miles to Happy Hunting Grounds. Hike another easy mile to While Ledge Camp where there is a junction with the Hurricane Deck Trail. Stay right at the junction and follow a creek down from camp. You ascend briefly, then continue down the Manzana Trail 2.8 miles, passing Lonnie Davis Camp, to reach South Fork Camp on the Sisquoc.

TOPOS: *Hurricane Deck, Peak Mountain,* W/A

STONE HOUSE (4,500′)(3.5) Set on a chaparral and pine flat near the confluence of Piru and Mutau creeks, this camp is furnished with two stoves. It is reachable by a trail that has suffered much flood damage.

From Lockwood Roadhead follow the Piru Creek Trail (20W07) southwest upstream for 2.9 miles. Be prepared for several stream crossings. At the junction with the Mutau Creek Trail (20W30) turn left, cross Piru Creek, and continue south on this lateral 0.6 miles to the camp.

TOPOS: *Lockwood Valley, McDonald Peak.*

SYCAMORE (2,000′)(12.7) Ironically, oak not sycamore trees stand guard over the bend in the Sisquoc where this grassy wilderness camp has been placed. It is just upstream from the junction of the Sisquoc and Jackson trails and has three stoves and an abundance of water.

From McPherson Roadhead follow the Sierra Madre Fire Road (32W13) southeast 7 miles toward Painted Rock. Just before reaching that camp turn right (southwest) to reach a junction at Montgomery Spring. Observing the signs, follow the overgrown road that is the Jackson Trail (27W05) over a low ridge that is lush with wildflowers in spring.

The Jackson Trail then descends steeply through chaparral and brush to reach the Sisquoc River in 5.5 miles. Cross the river, turn left (east) and continue across a flat to another crossing at the campsite in 0.2 miles.

TOPOS: *Hurricane Deck, Peak Mountain.* W/A

THE PINES (3,260′)(3.0) Set on a high pine-forested flat on the south slope of Chief Peak, this camp has been destroyed more than once by fire. It most recently suffered damage in the 1985 Wheeler Fire. The area has been consistently watched over and replanted by the thoughtful students of the Thatcher School. It features three stoves, and water is available all year from a nearby spring.

From Thacher Roadhead, follow the Horn Canyon Fire Road (5N10), then the Horn Canyon Trail (22W08), steeply uphill for 2.7 miles to the camp. The trail continues uphill from here to the Sisar Fire Road (4N15) in a steep 3.4 miles.

TOPO: *Ojai*

THREE MILE (5,850′)(8.5) Shaded by ponderosa pine and incense cedar this camp high on Piedra Blanca Creek offers the hardy backpacker three fire rings. The water supply from the stream is reliable.

From Reyes Peak Roadhead hike downhill on the Pine Mountain Trail (23W04) 5.8 miles to Haddock Camp as described above. Then continue down Piedra Blanca Creek on the Piedra Blanca Trail (22W03) for 2 miles to Three Mile Camp. Snow is sometimes a visitor here in winter.

TOPOS: *Lion Canyon, Reyes Peak, San Guillermo*

TWIN FORKS (3,650′)(2.4) If you're one of those backcountry travelers who have learned to let the music of falling water magically lull away their cares, you should definitely visit Twin Forks in the springtime. The camp is set on a sunny flat above the confluence of the north and middle forks of Piedra Blanca Creek, where the sound of cascading water permeates the air. There are three campsites here.

From the roadhead at Lion Campground follow the instructions provided 2.1 miles to Piedra Blanca Camp. Continue upstream on the Piedra Blanca Trail (22W03) 0.3 miles to this cool, oak-shaded camp. From Twin Forks, the trail climbs steeply up to Pine Mountain Lodge.

TOPO: *Lion Canyon*

UPPER BLUE CANYON (1,950′)(0.9) If you live in the Santa Barbara area and are seeking a destination for a spring dayhike or an early summer picnic, you've got one. With two stoves and a rustic table, this little camp is nestled in a green, wooded hollow, less than an hour's drive from downtown and less than a mile from the road. A fairly reliable stream runs through camp.

From Blue Canyon Roadhead follow the easy, winding Blue Canyon Trail (26W12) downstream for just under a mile to the camp. The blue-green rock formations you'll notice in the canyon walls are of the mineral serpentine, or soapstone, the state rock of California. The soft rock was carved by the Chumash Indians into useful stone implements.

TOPO: *Carpinteria*

UPPER RANCHO NUEVO (4,050′)(4.8) Nestled deep in a remote canyon on a streamside flat, this camp is flanked by steep walls where bigcone spruce, piñon pine, yucca, and chaparral varieties find their home. Water is available from the creek in the wet months when the surrounding peaks are frequently dusted by winter storms. Facilities include four stoves.

From Rancho Nuevo Roadhead follow the Rancho Nuevo Trail (24W03) upstream 1.4 miles past a register, mineral spring, and through

several stream crossings to Deal Junction Camp. Continue easily up the Rancho Nuevo Trail 3.4 miles to Upper Rancho Nuevo Camp.
TOPO: *Rancho Nuevo Creek.* W/A

UPPER REYES (4,700′)(3.5) Named for a local pioneer family and located in a cool canyon where the Beartrap Trail crosses Reyes Creek, this camp contains four stoves and a table. Because of its sheltered location, it offers pleasant camping most of the year, although the area can get quite hot in summer. Fishing, in season, is popular, though not always successful, along the reliable creek.

From Reyes Creek Roadhead follow the Beartrap Trail (23W02) uphill through chaparral. Stay left at a junction with a spur trail ascending from private Scheideck Camp and continue on a moderate ascent with a few patches of shade provided by stately bigcone spruce sentinels. In 2.5 miles you top a saddle and then descend an easy 1 mile to cross Reyes Creek and enter the camp.
TOPO: *Reyes Peak*

UPPER SANTA YNEZ (2,950′)(5.2) Situated near an open, grassy flatland near the headwaters of the Santa Ynez River, this seldom-visited camp, named for Saint Agnes of Assisi, ahs only a single stove. Water is seasonal here.

From Juncal Roadhead follow the Santa Ynez Fire Road (5N13) up past Juncal Dam and Jameson Lake. The Forest Service assures me the "no trespassing" signs do not apply to hikers on the closed road. Hike on the road (also numbered 27W07) up to reach Upper Santa Ynez Camp in 5.2 miles. By continuing another mile and a half farther on, you can top the Murietta Divide. From there, Divide Peak (4,707 feet) to the south-southwest can be easily climbed in a mile of extra hiking for outstanding views of Santa Barbara County and out to the vast Pacific.
TOPOS: *White Ledge Peak, Carpinteria.* F/C

UPPER SISQUOC FALLS (4,720′)(15.0) This small attractive camp along the Sisquoc Trail is not marked on most maps, yet it has much to offer. It's located 0.6 miles downstream from Lower Bear Camp at the foot of the steep Devil's Slide. Just above camp, the Sisquoc

River tumbles over some cliffs in a beautiful waterfall. Bigcone spruce and oaks shade this streamside camp with only a single stove.

From Santa Barbara Canyon Roadhead, follow the directions given above 13.7 miles to Bear Camp. From Bear follow the Sisquoc Trail (27W07) 0.7 miles past Lower Bear Camp, then 0.6 miles down the Devil's Slide to the foot of Sisquoc Falls.

TOPOS: *Big Pine Mountain, Salisbury Potrero, Fox Mountain, Madulce Peak.* W/A, F/C

UPPER TINTA (4,500′)(5.0) Located on the desert slope of 5,875-foot Cuyama Peak is an area of scrub oak, sagebrush, and scattered piñon pine, Upper Tinta is not a popular destination for backpackers. There is no water available here. You might want to hike an extra 2 miles up to the lookout atop Cuyama Peak for a wide-ranging view of the arid badlands area.

From Tinta Roadhead hike uphill out of the campground on the Tinta Trail (24W02). It follows Tinta Creek on a 3.6-mile moderate trek up to the Brubaker Canyon Fire Road (7N04). Turn left on the road and hike the remaining 1.4 miles to Upper Tinta Camp.

TOPOS: *Rancho Nuevo Creek, Cuyama Peak*

WATER CANYON (1,320′)(12.1) This old hunter's camp on the Sisquoc River with two stoves is set on a large flat under oak trees at the confluence of Water Canyon and the river. Water for fishing and swimming is ample.

From the NIRA Roadhead follow the detailed directions provided to Manzana Schoolhouse Camp (7.8 miles). Continue southeast onto the sandy Sisquoc Trail (30W12) on an uphill hike. You will find it washed out in several places, but the route upcanyon is always obvious, often marked by cairns. You will also notice remnants of turn-of-the-century settlements—bleached fence posts, rock foundations, rusted equipment—on the 4-mile trek to the camp and probably encounter a few head of grazing cattle.

TOPOS: *Bald Mountain, Zaca Lake*

WEST FORK LION (3,480′)(2.3) Formerly known as Dynamite Camp, this site on the West Fork of Lion Creek has four stoves, a single table, and can accomodate a large group. Bigcone spruce shade the flat here and water can be counted upon except in the driest months. The fire damage in the area is a result of the 1971 Bear Fire.

From Middle Lion Roadhead, follow the well-marked Topatopa Trail (22W06) easily up Lion Canyon to Four Points Trail Junction. The trail to the left goes to East Fork Lion Camp, the one straight ahead to Topatopa Ridge. Your route bears right to reach camp in 0.3 miles. You'll find a small waterfall beyond the camp.

TOPO: *Lion Canyon*

WHITE LEDGE (Santa Barbara County)(3,200´)(11.5) This small and attractive wilderness campsite with two stoves is located at the head of White Ledge Canyon at the junction of the Hurricane Deck and Manzana trails. The camp is shaded by a small forest of digger pines. Reliable White Ledge Creek runs past the site, and there are some fine large swimming holes for your enjoyment about half a mile downstream.

From the NIRA Roadhead, follow the detailed instructions I've provided 6.2 miles to Manzana Camp. From there, follow the Manzana Trail (30W13) 1.2 miles upstream through the Narrows to a trail junction. Bear left and follow an exposed switchbacking trail moderately uphill to the top of Hurricane Deck, then continue down to Happy Hunting Grounds Camp, 3.1 miles. From there it is an easy 1 mile hike to White Ledge.

TOPOS: *Hurricane Deck, San Rafael Mountain, Figueroa Mountain, Bald Mountain.* W/A

WHITE LEDGE (Ventura County)(3,750´)(5.6) Shaded by live oaks, this camp in Sisar Canyon is cool and pleasant in spring. Stream water is generally reliable and two stoves can be counted upon.

From Sisar Canyon Roadhead in the Upper Ojai Valley, hike past the locked gate onto the Sisar Canyon Fire Road (4N15) and follow it on a moderate ascent for 2.8 miles, staying at all road intersections. Just before the road begins its third switchback, turn onto the Red Reef Trail (21W08) on the right and ascend steeply for 2.8 miles to White Ledge. From the camp, the trail continues on over the Topatopa Ridge and down Red Reef Canyon to Sespe Creek.

TOPOS: *Ojai, Santa Paula Peak*

VII

THE ROADHEADS

A roadhead is the place where you park your car and start walking. Also referred to as "trailheads" or "roadends," they may occur at the end of a road or at any place where a trail crosses an automobile throughway. All the roadheads described below are accessible to passenger cars under dry conditions. It is unwise, however, to attempt to drive dirt roads during or soon after rainstorms.

In winter, the snow will close high-altitude roads such as the Pine Mountain and Sierra Madre for considerable periods. Rain also turns many dirt roads, such as the Alamo Mountain and Grade Valley, into muddy messes. Even paved roads that cross the Santa Ynez River north of Santa Barbara are usually closed due to flooding. If there is any doubt about conditions, contact the nearest district ranger station (see address and phone numbers, page 175) for the latest information.

The names I've given to the following roadheads are derived from the nearest well-known point. They are listed in alphabetical order along with their elevation and all the driving directions you need to reach them. Car campgrounds are frequently located at or near roadheads. A Forest Service map, available for a small charge from any U.S.F.S. Office, will provide you with the location of these campgrounds along with a list of their facilities.

To help guide you to each roadhead with a minimum of confusion, I have provided driving directions to each from the nearest city or town. Seven different and easily located cities are used as starting points:

Solvang is a small tourist community designed on a Scandinavian theme located on CAL 246 five miles east of U.S. 101 in the Santa

155

Ynez Valley. It is 45 miles north of Santa Barbara and 40 miles southwest of Santa Maria.

Fillmore is a small citrus community accessible from Los Angeles by the CAL 126 turnoff from Interstate 5 north of Valencia, or via the CAL 126 turnoff from U.S. 101 near Ventura.

Frazier Park is a resort community near Mt. Piños located just off Interstate 5 north of Gorman at the top of "the Grapevine."

New Cuyama is a small, rural town in the arid Cuyama Valley. From Los Angeles take Interstate 5 north to the CAL 166 turnoff north of the Grapevine. Follow 166 west through Miracopa to New Cuyama. From Santa Barbara or Oxnard, take U.S. 101 to the CAL 33 turnoff in Ventura. Follow Highway 33 north through the National Forest to its junction with CAL 166 and turn left to New Cuyama.

Ojai is a rural artisians' city located at the junction of CAL 33 and 150 twenty miles north of Ventura.

Santa Barbara is an oceanside city 95 miles north of Los Angeles and 77 miles south of Santa Maria on U.S. 101.

Santa Maria is located amid cultivated hills 77 miles north of Santa Barbara and 29 miles south of San Luis Obisbo on U.S. 101.

ALAMO MOUNTAIN (6,750') From Frazier Park follow Interstate 5 south to the Gorman exit. Turn right from the offramp, then right onto the Peace Valley Road. Drive 1 mile west and turn left onto the dirt Hungry Valley Road (8N01) and follow it 5 miles south to the Gold Hill–Alamo Mountain Road (7N01). Turn right and follow Forest Road (7N01) for 13 dirt miles on a curvy uphill climb to a road junction on Alamo Mountain. Turn left and drive 2 miles to the Snowy Creek Trailhead (19W04) on the left.

ALISO PARK (2,750') From New Cuyama travel northwest on State Highway 166 for 2.5 miles. Turn left onto the oiled Aliso Canyon Road and follow the signs for 6 miles to Aliso Park Campground. No water available here.

BALLARD (3,200') From Solvang take U.S. 101 north for 6 miles to the junction with CAL 154. Turn right and follow 154 to Los Olivios. Turn left onto the Figueroa Mountain Road (7N07) and follow it 10 miles to the U.S. Forest Service Figueroa Field Station. The roadhead is located on the left, 0.4 miles beyond the station and directly opposite the turnoff for the Tunnell Road, which is on the right.

BEAR CANYON (1,050′) From Santa Maria take CAL 166 east to the right-hand turnoff for the Tepusquet Road. Continue south on this winding country highway for 9 miles, watching on the left for a small sign marking Colson Canyon Road (11N04). Turn left and follow this dirt road, which is impassable in wet weather, past the Colson Campground and a few miles farther to a junction on La Brea Creek near the Webber Ranch where the Bear Canyon Trail (31W05) begins. Park off private property.

BIG CALIENTE (1,800′) From State Street in Santa Barbara turn northeast onto Los Olivos Street and contine onto Mountain Drive. Continue onto the Gibralter Road (5N25) and follow it to East Camino Cielo. Turn right and follow the road down to Juncal Campground. At Juncal, cross the river and follow the Santa Ynez River Road (5N15) west to the U.S. Forest Service Pendola Field Station. Turn right onto Road 5N16 and drive to the parking area at Big Caliente. High water closes this road at Juncal Campground in winter.

BLUE CANYON (2,100′) From State Street in Santa Barbara turn northeast onto Los Olivios Street and continue onto Mountain Drive. Continue onto the Gibralter Road (5N25), which you follow up to East Camino Cielo (5N12). Turn right and drive east over Cold Spring and Romero saddles to the signed beginning of the Blue Canyon Trail, on the left just before Blue Canyon Pass.

BLUE POINT (1,140′) From Fillmore take CAL 126 east for 8 miles. Bear left at the signed Piru turnoff and drive 1.5 miles into Piru. Follow the signs in town toward the Santa Felicia Dam and continue north on the Piru Canyon Road (4N13) for 13 miles past Lake Piru to Blue Point Campground. The last 5 miles are dirt and gravel.

CACHUMA SADDLE (3,100′) From Solvang take CAL 246 east 6 miles to its junction with CAL 154. Continue straight and bear left after 2 miles onto the Happy Canyon Road (7N07). Drive up this narrow, winding, but paved road, which becomes the Sunset Valley Road, to the U.S. Forest Service Field Station at Cachuma Saddle.

CERRO NOROESTE (MT. ABEL) (8,200') From New Cuyama follow CAL 166 approximately 15 miles east, to the junction with Forest Highway 95. Turn right and follow this paved and winding highway to the roadhead, on the right, 0.3 miles short of the roadend at the mountain's summit. Snow is not removed from this road during winter, and it is sometimes closed in winter by a locked gate at Apache Saddle.

CHERRY CREEK (4,850') From Ojai, take CAL 33 north for 27 miles. Turn left onto the dirt Cherry Creek Road (6N01) and continue on it for 3.5 miles, through the campground, onto the locked gate 1 mile beyond. This road has in the past been closed by frequent washouts where it crosses Sespe Creek during the winter months.

CHORRO GRANDE (4,100') From Ojai take CAL 33 north for 25 miles. The signed trailhead is on the right, 2.5 miles before Pine Mountain Inn.

COLD SPRING SADDLE (3,450') From State Street in Santa Barbara turn northeast onto Los Olivos Street and continue onto Mountain Drive. Continue onto the Gibralter Road (5N25) to East Camino Cielo. Turn right and drive on the paved road 4 miles to the signed roadhead at the Saddle.

COLSON (2,200') From Santa Maria take CAL 166 east to the right-hand turnoff for the Tepusquet Road. Continue on this winding country highway for 9 miles, watching on the left for the small sign that marks Colson Canyon Road (11N04). Turn left and follow this dirt road, which is impassable in wet weather, for about 6 miles. The roadhead is located 0.4 miles beyond the Colson Campground at a saddle directly opposite the point where a dirt mining road turns off to the left.

DOUGH FLAT (2,800') From Fillmore take Goodenough Road north for 3.5 miles and bear right at the "Y" in the road (the left spur dead ends) onto dirt Squaw Flat Road (6N16). Follow this dusty and winding route 11.5 miles to the locked gate at Dough Flat. Hikers should park at the small lot provided for the Alder Creek Trail. This road is muddy and impassable after wet weather.

FERNDALE RANCH (1,000´) From Ojai follow CAL 150 east for 9 miles to a wide turnout just below the Ferndale Ranch. The ranch is marked by a large sign posted on the green gates on the north side of the highway. Follow the paved road to the right of the ranch gates up the hill to the trailhead.

GAVIOTA (100´) From Santa Barbara follow U.S. 101 first west then north through Gaviota Pass. Then take the Lompoc/Vandenberg/CAL 1 offramp. Turn right then right again and continue to the parking area where the road ends. Please be aware that this portion of Gaviota State Park closes at sunset.

GRIDLEY CANYON (1,120´) From Ojai take State Highway 150 east. Turn left onto the Gridley Road (the second street past the Ranger Station). Follow the Gridley Road north 1.5 miles. The signed roadhead is on the left a short distance after you cross a bridge.

HARDLUCK (2,800´) From Frazier Park take Interstate 5 south to the Hungry Valley offramp. Turn west, then north, and continue less than a mile to a sharp bend in the road. Turn left here onto dirt Forest Road 8N02 and follow it for 3.5 miles to a junction with Forest Road 7N08. Turn left and follow the winding road for a slow 5 miles to Hardluck Campground. This road is impassable after winter rains.

JUNCAL (1,950´) From State Street in Santa Barbara, follow Los Olivos Street northeast to Mountain Drive. Continue on Mountain to Gibralter Road (5N25) and follow Gibralter up to the top of the Santa Ynez Mountains. Turn right onto East Camino Cielo (5N12) and follow it down to Juncal Campground on the Sant Ynez River.

LA CUMBRE (3,850´) From State Street in Santa Barbara turn northeast on Los Olivos Street and continue on to Mountain Drive. Follow Mountain Drive to the Gibralter Road 5N25 and continue to East

Camino Cielo. Turn left and drive on the paved road 2 miles to the signed trailhead for La Cumbre Vista Point.

LION CAMPGROUND (3,000′) From Ojai take CAL 33 north 14 miles. Turn right onto the graveled Rose Valley Road (6N31) and continue east for 6 miles to Lion Campground. The roadhead is at the point where Road 6N31 crosses Sespe Creek. During the winter months, the road is sometimes closed at a junction 1 mile south of Lion Campground.

LION SPRING (2,300′) From New Cuyama travel south on Perkins Road. You soon come to a "Y" in the road where you stay left, and then continue on through the oil fields. Bear left into Lion Spring Canyon, and left again to cross a small bridge. Finally bear left once again to a small parking area. The trailhead is located back down the road at that last "Y," where you bore left. A sign there reads "authorized vehicles only, Johnson Ranch" and marks the beginning of your route. Follow these directions carefully as it's easy to get lost in the many roads through the Arco oil field.

LOCKWOOD (5,000′) From Frazier Park follow the Frazier Road west for 3 miles. Bear left at the "Y" near Lake Of The Woods, and continue on the Lockwood-Ozena Road (9N03) for 5.5 miles to the Lockwood Creek Road on the left. Follow dirt Forest Road 8N12 for 1 mile to the locked gate. This last mile of road is not advised for travel during the winter months.

LOWER COLD SPRINGS (750′) From Santa Barbara take U.S. 101 South (really east) to San Ysidro Road. Turn left and follow San Ysidro to Mountain Drive. Turn left and follow Mountain to the roadhead, located where the creek crosses the road adjacent 895 Mountain Drive. Please observe the parking restrictions.

MATILIJA (1,540′) From Ojai take CAL 33 north for 5 miles. Turn left onto the paved Matilija Lake Road (5N13) and follow it another 5 miles to the locked gate at the roadend. Although the Matilija Road is labeled "Local Traffic Only," it is regularly driven by hikers.

McPHERSON (5,680 ′) From Santa Maria follow CAL 166 east to the Sierra Madre–Miranda Pine Mountain Road (32S13) 10 miles beyond the Pine Canyon Ranger Station. Turn right onto this winding dirt and gravel road and follow it for 27 miles to the locked gate near McPherson Peak. This road is closed in wet weather.

MIDDLE LION (3,140 ′) From Ojai take CAL 33 north for 14 miles. Turn right onto the graveled Rose Valley Road (6N31) and follow it for 5.5 miles to the unmarked dirt spur road above Lion Campground. Turn right and follow this spur 1 mile down to Middle Lion Campground. The trail begins at the point where the road crosses the creek.

MONO (1,590 ′) From State Street in Santa Barbara follow Los Olivos Street northeast and continue onto Mountain Drive. Follow Mountain to the Gibralter Road (5N25) and take Gibralter up to East Camino Cielo (5N12). Turn right and drive down to Juncal Campground, and here bear left onto the Romero-Camuesa Road (5N15). Continue west all the way to Mono Campground at Mono Debris Dam. High water in winter makes this backcountry route impassable beyond Juncal. Most of the hikes out of Mono begin a little beyond the campground at the locked gate near Little Caliente Hot Spring. There is some limited parking at that locked gate.

MOUNT PIÑOS (8,800 ′) From Frazier Park travel 3 miles west on the Frazier Mountain Road. Bear right at the ''Y'' near Lake Of The Woods then left onto the paved Mt. Piños Highway (9N24) and follow it uphill for 13.5 miles toward the Chula Vista Picnic Area. Just before reaching the picnic area, bear left onto a dirt road (closed in winter) and continue for 3 miles to the Condor Observation Point near the summit. Park here. In winter and inclement weather you'll have to hike the dirt road. Chains are required on the Mt. Piños Road in winter.

MUTAU FLAT (4,800 ′) From Frazier Park take the Frazier Mountain Road west for 3 miles, bearing left at the Lake Of The Woods ''Y.'' Continue on the Lockwood-Ozena Road (9N03) for 10.5 miles. Turn left onto the dirt Grade Valley Road (7N03) and continue for

12 miles, following the signs to Mutau Flat. Park at the end of the road, on the edge of the Flat. This road is closed by the Forest Service in winter.

NIRA (1,800′) From Solvang take CAL 246 east 6 miles to its junction with CAL 154. Continue straight ahead (east) but bear left after 2 miles onto Happy Canyon Road (7N07). Drive on this paved but winding route, which becomes Sunset Valley Road, over Cachuma Saddle, and follow it to its end at NIRA Campground. Space is provided at the east end of the campground for backpackers' parking.

NOJOQUI (1,000′) From CAL 246 in Solvang turn south on Alisal Road. Continue south then west on Alisal to the entrance to Nojoqui Falls County Park. Turn left and park at the end of the road.

ORTEGA (3,250′) From Ojai follow CAL 33 north for 9.5 miles. After passing Wheeler Gorge watch for the signed trailhead on the left side of the road.

OZENA (3,650′) From Ojai take CAL 33 north for approximately 37 miles. The signed beginning of the Deal Canyon Trail is located in a turnout on the left 0.8 miles before reaching the Ozena Ranger Station.

PINE FLAT (3,000′) From Santa Maria take CAL 166 east to the Miranda Pine–Sierra Madre Road (32S13) 10 miles beyond the Pine Canyon Ranger Station. Turn right and follow this dirt road 7 miles to a junction just past Miranda Pine Mountain. Turn right onto Forest Road 11N03 and follow it for 3 miles to the roadhead at the site of the old Pine Flat Campground. This road is impassable in wet weather.

PINE MOUNTAIN SUMMIT (4,500′) From Ojai take State Highway 33 north for 32 miles to the pass called Pine Mountain Summit. Park in the large turnout at Highway 33's junction with the Pine Mountain Road (6N06).

RANCHO NUEVO (3,520′) From Ojai take State Highway 33 north for 39.5 miles. Turn left onto the signed, dirt Tinta Canyon Road

(7N04A) and follow it across the usually dry Cuyama Riverbed 1.5 miles to Rancho Nuevo Campground. Be sure to stay left at a "Y" in the road. During and after rain, the river crossing is not passable.

RATTLESNAKE (900') From State Street in Santa Barbara turn north on Mission Canyon Road. Turn right briefly onto Foothill Road, then turn left again onto Mission following the signs toward the Botanical Gardens. Turn right onto Las Canoas Road and continue to the signed trailhead on the left located at a stone bridge over Rattlesnake Creek just shy of the entrance to Skofield Park. Park off the pavement.

REDROCK (1,100') From Santa Barbara follow CAL 154 north over San Marcos Pass. Turn right onto Paradise (Santa Ynez) Road (5N18) and follow this paved route for 10 miles and through several river crossings to the large parking area at the end of the road.

REYES CREEK (3,960') From Ojai take CAL 33 north for 37.5 miles. Turn right onto the paved Lockwood-Ozena Road (9N03) and follow it for 3.5 miles. Turn right onto the Reyes Creek Road (7N11) and continue across the Cuyama River to Reyes Campground in 2 miles.

REYES PEAK (6,800') From Ojai, drive north on CAL 33 for 32 miles to Pine Mountain Summit. Turn right onto the dirt Pine Mountain Road (6N06) and follow it 5 miles to Reyes Peak Campground. Trails for Chorro Grande, McGuire, and Raspberry Spring begin here. Hikers bound for Haddock and points beyond should keep driving east on the road to a locked gate. This road is closed in winter.

ROMERO SADDLE (2,750') From State Street in Santa Barbara, turn northeast onto Los Olivos Street. Follow Los Olivos to Mountain Drive and Mountain to Gibralter Road (5N25). Continue up Gibralter to East Camino Cielo (5N12) to turn right and follow it for 7 miles to the signed trailhead at Romero Saddle.

ROQUE (4,720') From Santa Maria follow CAL 166 east to the Miranda–Sierra Madre Road (32S13), 10 miles past the Pine Canyon Ranger Station. Turn right and follow the dirt Sierra Madre Road

(32S13) for 11.5 miles to the signed roadhead on the right. Wet weather closes this road.

ROSE VALLEY (3,400′) From Ojai follow CAL 33 morth 14 miles to the signed Rose Valley Road (6N31). Turn right and follow the Rose Valley Road 3 miles, watching for the signs to Rose Valley Campround. Turn right, continue a short distance, and park in or near the campground. The trail begins at a sign near campsite #4.

SAGE HILL (1,000′) From Santa Barbara, follow CAL 154 up and over San Marcos Pass. Turn right onto the Paradise (Santa Ynez) Road (5N18) and follow it to the Santa Barbara District Ranger Station. Turn left and drive across the Santa Ynez River bearing first right, then left, through the campground to the signed trailhead. High water may close this river crossing in winter.

SAN ROQUE (450′) From U.S. 101 in Santa Barbara, take the Los Positas Road offramp. Turn north and continue onto San Roque Road. Follow San Roque to its end at the Cater Filtration Plant. Park in the spaces provided.

SANTA BARBARA CANYON (3,540′) From New Cuyama take CAL 166 east for about 5 miles to Kirschenmann Road. Turn south and follow Kirschenmann to Foothill Road. Turn left and follow Foothill to Santa Barbara Canyon Road. Turn right and follow this road up the canyon past the Santa Barbara Canyon Ranch to Cox Flat. Park near the locked gate by the trailhead and off signed private property.

SANTA YNEZ (1,120′) From Santa Barbara take CAL 154 north over San Marcos Pass. Turn right onto the Paradise (Santa Ynez) Road (5N18) and continue about 9 miles to the roadhead on the right, marked by a sign indicating Trail 27W25, 1 mile beyond Santa Ynez Campground. High water closes this road in winter.

SESPE GORGE (3,750′) From Ojai take CAL 33 north for 25 miles. Just after driving through narrow Sespe Gorge, a popular spot for rock climbers, watch on the right for a sign near a small bridge indicating the Potrero John Trail.

SISAR CANYON (1,800′) From Ojai take CAL 150 east for 8 miles. Turn left at the Summit School onto the Sisar Road and follow it north for a bumpy mile to the locked gate at the forest boundary. When the Sisar Canyon Road turns to dirt, stay right, then left, then right at the intersections you encounter.

SNYDER (2,960′) From Santa Barbara follow the San Marcos Pass Road, CAL 154 north to San Marcos Pass. Turn right onto East Camino Cielo and drive east three miles to saddle. The locked gate marking your trailhead is immediately to the north.

THACHER (1,400′) From Ojai follow CAL 150 east for 1.5 miles to Reeves Road. Bear left onto Reeves and continue 1 mile to McAndrew Road. Turn left and drive through the entrance to the Thacher School property at the corner of McAndrew and Thacher roads. Continue on to the school property and keep bearing right to the locked gate on the east side of the campus where a sign marks the beginning of the Horn Canyon Trail.

THORN MEADOWS (4,750′) From Frazier Park take the Frazier Mountain Road west for 3 miles to the Lake Of The Woods "Y." Bear left and continue 10.5 miles on the Lockwood-Ozena Road (9N03). Turn left onto the dirt Grade Valley Road (7N03) and follow it for 7.5 miles. Turn right onto the Thorn Meadows spur road (7N03B) and follow it for 0.5 miles to the beginning of the Cedar Creek Trail (22W10) on the right. This road is muddy and impassable in winter.

THREE FALLS (5,400′) From Frazier Park take the Frazier Mountain Road 3 miles west to the Lake Of The Woods "Y." Bear left here onto the Lockwood-Ozena Road (9N03) and continue for 8 miles to Boy Scout Road. Turn right and follow this paved road for 2.5 miles to the gate at the entrance to Three Falls Boy Scout Camp. Permission is required to park on or cross the property.

TIMBER CANYON (2,040′) From Fillmore take CAL 126 west for 5 miles. Turn right onto the dirt Timber Canyon Road and follow it for 4.5 miles to the locked gate at the forest boundary.

TINTA (3,650′) From Ojai take CAL 33 north for 39.5 miles. Turn left onto the signed dirt Tinta Canyon Road (7N4A) and follow it across the usually dry Cuyama riverbed 1 mile to a "Y". Turn right and continue the remaining 2 miles to Tinta Campground. The crossing of the Cayuma River here is impossible after rains.

TUNNEL (1,000′) From State Street in Santa Barbara turn north onto Alamar Road. Turn right onto Foothill Road, then left onto Mission Canyon. Bear left at a "Y" onto Tunnel Road and follow it to its end. Be sure to observe the "No Parking" signs in the area as offenders are often cited.

UPPER COLD SPRING (1,900′) From State Street in Santa Barbara turn north onto Las Olivos Street and continue onto Mountain Drive. Follow Mountain to the Gibralter Road (5N25). Continue on Gibralter approximately 3 miles to a wide turnout on the right, site of a now-banned target-shooting area, where the West Fork Cold Spring Trail (27W16) begins.

UPPER OSO (1,000′) From Santa Barbara take CAL 154 over San Marcos Pass. Turn right onto the Paradise (Santa Ynez) Road (5N18) and follow it east for 5.5 miles. Just after the first river crossing turn left onto the paved Oso Road (5N15) and follow it 1 mile to Upper Oso Campground. Parking is provided for backpackers.

UPPER RATTLESNAKE (2,450′) From State Street in Santa Barbara turn northeast onto Los Olivos Street and continue onto Mountain Drive. Follow Mountain to Gibralter Road (5N25) and continue uphill. Drive into the Santa Ynez Mountains approximately 4 miles to the signed upper end of the Rattlesnake Trail on the left. Be sure to park off the pavement.

VAN TREE (680′) From Fillmore follow Grand Avenue north to its end at the locked dirt road at the Van Tree Ranch. Permission is required to pass across the ranch property.

ZACA LAKE (2,400') From Solvang, take CAL 246 west to U.S. 101. Follow 101 north for 7 miles. Turn right onto the Zaca Road (signed for Zaca Station) and continue on this paved road for 5 miles. Turn right onto Forest Road 8N11 where a sign points to Zaca Lake. Continue on this narrow winding road 6 miles to the resort. This is private land and a nominal charge is made for parking. Be sure to check in at the lodge office. You may phone ahead for parking reservations.

VIII

TIPS FOR ENVIRONMENTALLY
SAFE CAMPING

THE WILDERNESS ETHIC

Wild backcountry areas today are at a premium. They can remain wild and unspoiled for future generations to appreciate and enjoy only if they are protected and cared for by those who use them today. To minimize environmental impact as much as possible, wilderness travelers must make every effort "to camp and leave no trace."

CAMPSITES whenever possible, should be 100 feet from streambanks. This is especially important to remember when camping outside of established trail camps. Camping away from streambanks ensures a warmer camp, protects fragile vegetation, prevents possible pollution, and provides some protection in the event of a flash flood. Try to camp on mineral soil, not in meadows or on potreros, to cut down on damage to growing things. The Forest Service encourages the use of the established campsites mentioned in this book to concentrate environmental impact and to minimize it elsewhere. Currently, in the San Rafael and Dick Smith wilderness areas, bivouacking is not allowed. There you must overnight in a trail camp.

Here are a few tips for conscientious camping:

Any type of camp craft building, whether for kitchen emplacements or bedsites is destructive to backcountry areas.

Never cut boughs for bedding; use a lightweight foam pad instead.

Do not put nails in trees; this is a starting point for disease.

To avoid disturbing the soil with drainage trenches, locate your camp so rainwater will drain away naturally.

When breaking camp, erase all possible evidence that you were there.

FIRES should be kept small and to a minimum. Fires at trail camps must be confined to the camp stoves provided. When camping outside of designated sites, follow the instructions in the pamphlet provided by the Forest Service and available at any Ranger Station. Most times of the year, a Fire Permit will be required. These are free, and are available by mail from the U.S.F.S. Office in Goleta or from a District Ranger Station.

Rotting down wood provides a natural fertilizer for the forest floor and helps keep it verdant. It is a significant link in the forest ecosystem. Since wood has become rare in many of the more popular camps of the Los Padres, the use of a lightweight backpacking stove for cooking is strongly recommended. A Campfire Permit is required for the use of these stoves in all backcountry areas during the summer fire season (July 1 to the first winter rains).

Plan to build fires with down wood only. Standing wood, living or dead, should not be cut.

Never leave your fire unattended and, when breaking camp, drown it completely, stir the ashes, and drown it again until everything is cold to the touch.

SANITATION has been provided for by nature. There is a system of biological disposers in the top six to eight inches of the soil that works to decompose organic material and human waste. If there are no toilet facilities in the area, use a small latrine trowel to dig a hole no more than ten inches in diameter and no deeper than six inches. Cover everything completely. Fill the hole with loose soil and tramp it down. Heavy spring runoff carries with it any uncovered human waste. This is one of the ways in which wilderness water sources become polluted. Try to locate latrine sites at least 150 feet away from the nearest water source and away from all dry watercourses.

Burying trash is illegal. The practice was formerly promoted as an acceptable substitute for littering. But today, too many people are visiting the backcountry, and experience has shown that animals often dig up buried articles.

When traveling, put candy wrappers, orange peels, and the like in your pocket or pack for later disposal. In camp, burn everything that will burn (paper and plastic) if you build a fire. Aluminum foil, cans, and bottles do not burn. They will not decay in your lifetime. Try to repack food in plastic bags before you hit the trail so you won't have to carry in unburnable containers. If you must bring them in, you will *have to* carry them out. Leftover edibles should be burned completely. Make a conscious effort to leave your campsite cleaner than you found it. When in doubt, pack it out.

ANIMALS will not harm you unless they are provoked or frightened. A form of provocation, especially where rattlesnakes are concerned, includes stepping on them. Watch where you step when walking and where you put your hands while climbing. To guard against a trip ruined by rodents, suspend you food at night from a tree, high above the ground and away from limbs. There are still a few bears and many many rodents in this backcountry.

WATER should be drawn, whenever possible, upstream from any trail crossing used by pack stock to guard against contamination.

Prevent pollution by keeping even biodegradeable soap out of water sources. Do all your bathing, clotheswashing, and pot scrubbing well away from the banks of streams, using a lightweight folding wash basin. When bathing, lather and rinse ashore.

Water drawn from backcountry streams should be considered polluted if it is not moving, looks "dirty," or is from the Santa Ynez or Sisquoc rivers, Piru or Sespe creeks. *Giardia* is rapidly becoming a problem in the watercourses of the Santa Barbara Backcountry, and the Forest Service cautions visitors against drinking water even from streams which appear to be clean and free-flowing. The only effective treatment for *giardia*-infected water is to boil it for five minutes or filter it through a straining device. Purification tablets are not effective against giardia.

TRAILS are expensive to build and maintain, especially switchbacks. Keep to the trail whenever possible. Cutting corners breaks down the edges and begins erosion and gullying. Dislodged rocks can injure people below.

Always use a compass and plan your route with a topographic map *and* a Forest Service map for safety. If you are traveling crosscountry, restrain the impulse to blaze trees or build cairns. The next hikers will enjoy finding their own way too.

On the trail, remember that pack stock always has the right of way because mules and horses are sometimes unpredictable and difficult to manage. When you see stock approaching, move off the trail to a spot where the animals can see you plainly, on the uphill side if possible, and wait quietly for them to pass.

INDIAN ARTIFACTS, except arrowheads and the like washed out along trails, are fully protected by the Federal Antiquities Act. Any new discovery that you think you may have stumbled upon should not be disturbed in any way. Mark the spot on your map, note the location, and report it to the Forest Archeologist at the U.S.F.S. Headquarters in Goleta.

BACKCOUNTRY TRAVELERS' CHECKLIST

Here is a list of the items you might want to bring along when hiking the Santa Barbara Backcountry. Although they range from the optional to the vitally important, selection depends upon your individual camping lifestyle. Please note that the items marked with astrisks should be considered essential for every overnight camping trip.

PACK*
MAP*
COMPASS*
BOOTS*
CLOTHING: thermal underwear, long pants, shorts, underwear, shirt, sweater, down jacket, down vest, poncho, rain jacket and pants, hat, bandana, mittens, socks, extra clothing*
CAMPFIRE PERMIT
FISHING EQUIPMENT AND LICENSE
FOOD
BEDDING: sleeping bag, foam pad, ground sheet, tent or tarp, tent stakes
FIRST AID: first aid kit*, insect repellent, chapstick, antacid, sunscreen, toothbrush, toothpaste, sunglasses*, water filtration kit, purification tablets, snake bite kit*, whistle, moleskin, foot powder, needle and thread, personal medication, eyeglasses
MISCELLANEOUS: toilet paper*, metal mirror, camera and film, lenses and filters, binoculars, waterproof matches*, cup, bowl, stove, fuel, knife*, utensils, candle or fire starter*, latrine trowel, biodegradeable soap, cooking pots, potholder, towel, notebook and

pencil, book for reading, flashlight*, extra bulbs and batteries*, nylon cord (35 to 50 feet), canteen*, emergency food*, GI can opener

ADDRESSES FOR CAMPFIRE PERMITS, MAPS, AND CAMPING INFORMATION

Campfire Permits can be obtained at any of the offices listed below. Mail applications for Campfire Permits should be sent to the Supervisor's Office. Allow at least one and one-half weeks for receipt of the permit.

(When phoning any forest office for conditions, information, or fire closure restrictions, ask for the Recreation Officer.)

A Campfire Permit is required when using any portion of the back-country during the summer months between July 1 and the first winter rains. The permit is also required to build a fire in the San Rafael or Dick Smith wilderness areas any time of the year *or* when camping anywhere in the National Forest outside of an established trail camp. The permit is free to anyone who agrees to follow the simple rules intended to protect the visitor and the forest resource. Only one permit is required for a group traveling together, and group size is limited to 25 peole. The permit is good for a single trip, during a specified period. A separate permit is necessary for each trip.

SUPERVISOR'S OFFICE
6144 Calle Real
Goleta, Ca. 93117
805-683-6711

Mt. Piños District
Chuchupate Ranger Station
Frazier Park, Ca. 93225
805-345-3731

Ojai District
1190 East Ojai Avenue
Ojai, Ca. 93023
805-646-4348

Santa Barbara District
Los Prietos Ranger Station
Star Route, Santa Ynez Canyon
Santa Barbara, Ca. 93105
805-967-3481

Santa Lucia District
1616 Carlotti Drive
Santa Maria, Ca. 93454
805-925-9538

BIBLIOGRAPHY

Blakely, E.R., and Barnette, Karen. *Historical Overview of the Los Padres National Forest*. Los Padres Interpretive Association, 1985.

Boy Scouts of America, *Camping Booklet—Ventura County*. Ventura County Council, 1971.

Brown, Vinson, and Lawrence, George. *The California Wildlife Region*. Healdsburg, Naturegraph, 1965.

Burtness, Robert. *A Camper's Guide to the Tri-County Area*. Mission Council, Boy Scouts of America, 5th Edition, 1984.

Crain, Jim, and Milne, Terry. *Camping Around California*. New York, Random House, 1976.

Ford, Ray, Jr., and Hiester, Marty. *Trails of the San Rafael Wilderness*. Santa Barbara, Granite Stairway Mountaineering, 1974.

Grant, Campbell. *Rock Paintings of the Chumash*. Berkeley, University of California Press, 1965.

Heizer, R.F., and Whipple, M.A., eds. *The California Indians—A Source Book*. Berkeley, University of California Press, 1973.

Heizer, R.F., ed. *Handbook of North American Indians, Volume 8—California*. Washington, Smithsonian Institution, 1978.

Jaeger, Edmund C., and Smith, Arthur C. *Introduction to the Natural History of Southern California*. Berkeley, University of California Press, 1971.

Jones, Charles, and Knab, Klaus. *American Wilderness*. San Jose, Gousha Publications, 1973.

McMillan, Ian. *Man and the California Condor*. New York, E.P. Dutton and Co., 1968.

Munz, Philip A. *California Desert Wildflowers*. Berkeley, University of California Press, 1962.

———. *California Mountain Wildflowers*. Berkeley, University of California Press, 1963.

———. *California Spring Wildflowers*. Berkeley, University of California Press, 1961.

Peterson, P. Victor. *Native Trees of Southern California*. Berkeley, University of California Press, 1966.

Raven, Peter H. *Native Shrubs of Southern California*. Berkeley, University of California Press, 1966.

Smith, Dick, and Van Schaik, Frank. *California's Backcountry— The Mountains and Trails of Santa Barbara County*. Santa Barbara, McNally and Loftin, 1962.

———. *Condor Journal*. Santa Barbara, Capra Press and the Santa Barbara Museum of Natural History, 1978.

INDEX

ABOUT THE AUTHOR

Dennis Gagnon is a freelance travel writer who has published articles on hiking in Colorado, Wyoming, Oregon, and throughout California. He is the author of *A Guide to the Theodore Solomons Trail,* a Yosemite-to-Mt. Whitney route that offers wilderness travelers through the Sierra Nevada an alternative to the over-used John Muir Trail. He has also written *Hike Los Angeles,* a two-volume comprehensive guide to the trails of the urban backcountry of the L.A. Basin. He is a regular contributor to the *California Explorer,* a monthly backpacker's newsletter. Dennis Gagnon hikes the trails of the West when he can and works in Hollywood as a television producer when he must.